ALABAMA FOOTPRINTS Confrontation

A Collection of
Lost & Forgotten Stories

Read more books of the The Alabama Footprints Series

ALABAMA FOOTPRINTS Exploration

ALABAMA FOOTPRINTS Settlement

ALABAMA FOOTPRINTS Pioneers

More coming soon!

Additional stories of Alabama pioneers can be found on the websites:

www.alabamapioneers.com

www.daysgoneby.me

Follow on Facebook at:

http://www.facebook.com/alabamapioneers

http://www.facebook.com/daysgonebyme

and

Twitter

http://twitter.com/alabamapioneers

ALABAMA FOOTPRINTS
Confrontation

A Collection of
Lost & Forgotten Stories

by

Donna R. Causey

Copyright © 2015 by Alabama Pioneers
All Rights Reserved
This book, or parts thereof, may not be reproduced in any form without permission
Published by Donway Publishing

ISBN - 13:978-1518702716

ISBN - 10:1518702716

DEDICATION
This book is dedicated to all
my friends and family in Alabama

INTRODUCTION

It's not easy to determine the first of a long chain of events which led to war with the Native Americans in Alabama, but one major factor was the construction of public roads. At first the Native Americans embraced the idea of a good road through the heart of their nation because of the benefits to them. Their chiefs gave their consent because a good road would make their commerce with the outside world easier and more profitable, so roads were quickly built.

However, some Native Americans disagreed with their chiefs decisions and quarrels developed within the Indian Nation which divided them into two fiercely antagonistic parties. While many agreed to the roads, others objected to the thoroughfare because of the large number of white immigrants who constantly passed through their country to regions beyond. They felt their chiefs had betrayed their interests by granting the right of way for the public road and complained bitterly that they would soon be walled up between white settlements on every side.

The land on the Tombigbee River had become heavily populated, but many Native Americans still retained hope of driving the whites away from the banks of that river and recover the territory to themselves.

Spanish settlers, who felt the land they lived on belonged to Spain, utilized the disagreements among the Native Americans and encouraged the anger of the Creeks who were already disposed to be unfriendly toward the Americans. Agents of the British added their voices to the quarrel. Emissaries of the British entered the Creek country, stirred up strife and sowed the seeds of future hostility. They sent secret messages to the Creeks promising arms, ammunition, and aid to the Creeks in the event of a war.

Thus the region of the future state of Alabama was ripe for turbulence in the spring of 1811 when Tecumseh made his journey to the south, accompanied with about thirty of his warriors. He came with the purpose of executing the formation of a great offensive and defensive alliance between the tribes of the North and those of the South against the Americans.

Visit http://alabamapioneers.com
for more unknown stories about the state of Alababama and follow on Facebook at
http://www.facebook.com/alabamapioneers
and
http://twitter.com/alabamapioneers

Table of Contents

Preparing For War 1
   Tecumseh's Visit 3
   Tecumseh Causes Earthquake 7
   William Weatherford – Red Eagle 9
   A Warning Saves Many Lives 13
   The Breaking Point 17
Revenge 23
   The Battle Of Burnt Corn 25
   Terrified Settlers Abandon Farms 29
Massacres 33
   Surprise Attack 35
   Survivor Stories From Fort Mims 39
   Kimball James Massacre & Fort Sinquefield 43
Chaos and Panic 49
   Pushmataha Offers Assistance 51
   Tennessee Responds To The Call 55
Major Battles 61
   Battle Of Tallaseehatchee 63
   Jackson Protects Friendly Creeks 67
   Hillabee Massacre 69
   Autosee Battle By Georgians 73
   Holy Ground Campaign And Battle 79
   Threat Of Starvation Men Turn To Mutiny 85
   General Coffee Is Wounded 95
   Entire Rear Guard, Panic-Stricken, Had Plunged Into The Stream 99
   Georgia Volunteers Fight At Calabee 103
The War Ends 107
   Horseshoe Bend 109
   The Surrender 121
   Red Eagle After The War 125
   Bibliography 131

Preparing For War

Tecumseh's Visit

It's a long journey from the region round the Great Lakes where Tecumseh lived to the shores of the Alabama and Tombigbee rivers.

The great northern chief had completed many deeds by which he won a reputation for the possession of genius, both as a soldier and as a statesman; but nothing in his history so certainly proves his title to rank among really great men as his boldness and brilliancy in planning the formation of a great confederacy of the tribes which extended in a chain from the lakes on the north to the Gulf of Mexico on the south.

Tecumseh wood carving ca. 1843 (Library of Congress)

He was wise enough to learn of his foes. He saw that their strength lay in the union; that it was by *joining all their camp-fires*, as he phrased it, that they made themselves irresistible; and as he saw with consternation that the great tide of white man was steadily advancing westward, he understood, as few men of his race did, that there was but one possible way to stop the encroaching stream. Separately they were powerless, because separately they could be beaten one by one. White troops who were engaged in reducing an Illinois tribe during one month could be sent the next to oppose another tribe in Mississippi or Alabama. Tecumseh realized that the secret of the white man's success lay in two facts; first that the whites were united, working together for a common purpose, and helping each other in turn; and second that the whites used the same troops over and over again to fight the separately acting tribes. Thus, Tecumseh conceived a plan to form a confederacy of all the Native American tribes from north to south to act together and oppose the advance of the white man.[1]

Tecumseh arrived in the south in 1811. He spent the first part of his journey with the Choctaws and the Chickasaws, but failed to win them to go along with his scheme so he made his way to Florida where he made easy converts of the warlike Seminoles.

In October of 1811, he arrived in Creek country and he marched into a Grand Council meeting at Tookabatcha that was being held by Colonel Hawkins, the American Indian Agent. Tecumseh and his warriors "were dressed in their most impressive savage costumes, consisting of very little else than buffalo tails and other ornaments,"[2] Their faces were painted black and their heads adorned with eagle plumes. They marched solemnly round and round the central square of the town.

He did not come as a stranger. The fame of his exploits in the North had reached the Creeks, and he was known to them even more favorably in another way. Nearly twenty-five years before, Tecumseh, had dwelt among the Creeks as a young man for about two years, and the stories of his feats as a hunter had lived after him as a tradition. When he came again in 1811, he was known as a great man of whose deeds they had heard stories about during their childhood.

---

[1] Red Eagle; or, Wars with the Indians of Alabama By George Cary Eggleston Ward. Lock, & Company, 1881 - Creek War, 1813-1814
[2] Red Eagle; or, Wars with the Indians of Alabama By George Cary Eggleston Ward. Lock, & Company, 1881 - Creek War, 1813-1814

When he had sufficiently impressed the audience with a proper sense of his dignity, he went through the most solemn ceremonies of friendship with his hosts and exchanged tobacco with them. Most of the chiefs received him with welcome friendship, but one chief, Captain Isaacs, rejected his overtures and shook his head when asked to shake hands. "He refused to exchange tobacco; and with the frankness of a brave man convinced of his duty, he told Tecumseh to his face that he was a bad man, and added, "You are no greater than I am."

While Colonel Hawkins was in the meeting, Tecumseh made no effort to put his plan into execution. Each day he appeared in the square to deliver his talk that all ears were anxious to hear it, but he remained silent. Instead, at the end of the day he would say, "I will make my talk tomorrow." Colonel Hawkins prolonged the council for a few days but still Tecumseh did not relate his purpose. Finally, Colonel Hawkins brought the conference to an end and departed. Once he left Tecumseh delivered his long speech, full of fire and vengeance.

Tecumseh informed the Creeks that they had made a fatal mistake by adopting the ways of the whites and becoming friendly with them. He encouraged them to abandon their plows, looms and cast off the garments which the whites had taught them to wear; to return to the condition and customs of their ancestors, and to be ready at command to become the enemies of the whites. He told them, "The whites have turned the beautiful forests into large fields, and stained the clear rivers with the washings of the soil and we would all be soon subjected to African servitude."

In his conclusion, he announced that the British, their former friends, had sent him from the Big Lakes, to procure their services to expel the Americans from all Indian soil and that the King of England was ready to handsomely reward all who would fight for his cause.

Next, a prophet, Tenskwatawa, who also happened to be Tecumseh's brother, spoke to the people. He had traveled with Tecumseh from Detroit. He said that he frequently communed with the Great Spirit and that the Great Spirit sent Tecumseh to their country upon this mission and declared that all those who joined the war party would be shielded from all harm and none would be killed in battle. He said that the Great Spirit would surround them with quagmires in which all the Americans would be swallowed up as they approached. Then he informed them that at a certain time they would see the arms of Tecumseh stretched like pale fire on the vault of heaven, and that would be the time to begin the war. (**Note**: It is believed that a British officer in Canada had told Tecumseh when a comet would appear, and Tecumseh used that as a sign to start the war.)

A short time before daylight the council adjourned with over more than half the audience resolved to go to war against the Americans.

Tecumseh Causes Earthquake

As Tecumseh continued to speak to the Native Americans throughout the southern United States, many warriors joined with him, but others doubted his promise of success. Many were infatuated by his persuasive eloquence and promised their allegiance to him and his cause, but at Tuckabatchie he faced resistance.

His remarks were not greeted with the same cordiality he had received elsewhere. Chief Big Warrior told him, "Promises are like the wind. The wind is free. Talk is nothing."

Tecumseh became angry and stamped his foot upon the ground, and he replied, "Your blood is white. You have taken my talk, and the sticks, and the wampum, and the hatchet, but you do not mean to fight. I know the reason. You do not believe the Great Spirit has sent me. You shall know. I leave Tuckabatchee directly and shall go straight to Detroit. When I arrive there, I will stamp on the ground with my foot, and shake down all the houses in Tuckabatchee."

A few weeks later, on December 16, 1811, the New Madrid Earthquake shook the United States, and a large tract of land on the Mississippi sank. It was so powerful that the Mississippi River reversed its southerly flow and threw riverboats against the shore.

Native American lodges trembled and shook, then suddenly toppled over. Every house in Tuckabatchee was demolished and the Alabama Indians believed it was Tecumseh's prophecy coming true.

Terrified and alarmed, the Creeks rushed wildly about, crying: "Tecumseh has arrived at Detroit. His threat has come true. We must join with him in his confederation or all will be lost."

Some believe that Tecumseh had heard from a white astrologer that an earthquake was soon to take place and used this information to his advantage. How much fact there is to the story we do not know, but stories will grow and the later versions of this story state that the earthquake took place on the very day of Tecumseh's arrival in Detroit.

No matter where the truth lies. The fact remains that warriors took up their rifles and prepared for war; prophets and witches became numerous, and murders were committed on the frontier. The earthquake secured for Tecumseh a great and lasting reputation.

However, Big Warrior, though sadly troubled, did not follow, and continued firm in his allegiance to the United States.

William Weatherford – Red Eagle

Among the Native Americans, Tecumseh found a bold, gifted, and eloquent leader named William Weatherford (also known as Lamochattee, Red Eagle, Hoponida Fulsahi, and Billy Larney[3]). His parents were Charles Weatherford, a thrifty Scottish peddler and Sehoy Marchand, daughter of the Tookabatcha chief. Sehoy was the widow of Colonel Tate (Tait), a British officer who had commanded Fort Toulouse and the half-sister of Alexander McGillivray. The Weatherfords became prosperous and owned a large plantation on the Alabama River where they had a store, farm and race-track.

Into this home of wealth, their son William was born ca. 1774. (**Note**: His exact birthdate is not known) He was well skilled in all the arts of hunting as well as the rudiments of war as practiced by his people. It was said that he stood six foot two inches tall and weighed around 175 pounds. Red Eagle was a rich planter who lived near the Holy Ground.

Alexander McGillivray (Alabama Department of Archives and History)

---

3 According to a family friend, Thomas S. Woodward, William Weatherford was not called Red Eagle until 1855 after a publication of A. B. Meek's poem, *The Red Eagle: A Poem of the South*, which was a lengthy romanticized tale based loosely on Weatherford and his exploits. Today William Weatherford is nearly universally called Red Eagle by writers even though it does not appear to have a basis in fact.

In the company of his uncles, Alexander McGillivray and LeClerc Milfort, he learned of the aggression of the whites and the wrongs they had committed against his mother's people. Wars with the Choctaws and Chickasaws, and occasional attacks on the whites, developed his military qualities and his matchless prowess.

An eloquent and passionate speaker, Weatherford heard Tecumseh at Tuckabatchee, but he counseled against Tecumseh's plans for war. Even when he discovered the irrepressible spirit of war working its doom among the Creeks, he still remained reluctant to war against the whites because his brother John, his half-brother David Tate, and others of his Native American blood were friendly to the whites.

But Red Eagle began to realize that the white man was rapidly multiplying in the Tombigbee area, and he knew that the Americans had made acquisitions of new territory which would still further invite American emigration into the neighborhood of the Creek Nation and he became alarmed. No matter on which side he fought he was bound to suffer so when the storm came on, he did not stand by as an idle watcher. He joined the Creeks.

When Tecumseh visited the Creeks, he took Red Eagle into his councils, and made him his confidant and principal fellow-worker. Red Eagle's knowledge of the Creeks helped Tecumseh win over more Native Americans to his cause. Acting upon Red Eagle's suggestion, Tecumseh used his prophet, Josiah Francis, to increase the numbers of the war party by ensuring their success through prophecies.

Still, Red Eagle hesitated to enter the war for sometime. He was eager for war between the Creeks and whites, but a war between a part of the Creeks on the one hand, and the rest of the Creeks with the whites on the other, a war in which he must fight his own brothers and his nearest friends, was a very different and much less attractive war.

"There was another reason of Red Eagle's hesitation at this time—perhaps a stronger cause than either of the others. He was in love, and his sweetheart was among the people whom he must fight if he fought at all. Weatherford was a rich planter, and lived at this time on a fine place near the Holy Ground, and being a young widower he had conceived a passionate fancy for one Lucy Cornells, a young girl of mixed Indian and white blood, who has been described by persons who knew her as very attractive and beautiful. However that may be, it is certain that Red Eagle's devotion to her was profound."

A Warning Saves Many Lives

In 1812, the long-threatened war between the United States and Great Britain was formally declared. At the beginning of the war, the Americans had asserted their title to the town and harbor of Mobile, which, although a part of the territory ceded many years before to the United States by the French, had until now been held by the Spanish.

The affair was so well managed that the place was surrendered without bloodshed and occupied by the American forces. However, its surrender created hostility among the Spanish in Florida, and even though America was at peace with Spain, the Spanish authorities at Pensacola readily lent themselves to the schemes of the British. In 1812, they had even allowed a British force to land at Pensacola, take possession of the fort there, and make it a base of operations against the United States.

The Spanish also assisted the Native Americans by providing parties of Indians who visited them to trade for arms and ammunition to use against Americans.

After Tecumseh's visit, a friendly Indian by the name of Sam Moniac was driven from his home and his cattle was taken to Pensacola to be sold by a marauding warring party. He hid in the swamps for awhile, then finally ventured out at night to visit his home. where he met High Head Jim who was at the head of some hostile Indians. In order to save his life, he lied and told the hostile party that he had given up his peaceful beliefs and had made up his mind to join the war party.

He related his frightening experience in the a deposition taken in 1813 as follows:

About the last of October, 1812, thirty northern Indians came down with Tecumseh, who said he had been sent by his brother, the Prophet. They attended our council at the Tuccabache, and had a talk for us. I was there for the space of three days; but every day, while I was there, Tecumseh refused to deliver his talk; and, on being requested to give it, said the sun had gone too far that day. The next day I came away, and he delivered his talk. It was not until about Christmas that any of our people began to dance the war-dance. The Muskhogees have not been used to dance before war, but afterward. At that time, about forty of our people began this "northern custom;" and my brother-in-law, Francis, who also pretends to be a "prophet," was at the head of them.

Their number has very much increased since, and there are probably now more than one half of the Creek nation who have joined them. Being afraid of the consequences of a murder having been committed on the mail-route, I left my house on the road, and had gone down to my plantation on the river, where I remained some time. I went to Pensacola with some steers; during which time my sister and brother, who have joined the war party, came and took off a number of my horses, and other stock, and thirty-six of my negroes. About twenty-two days ago I went up to my house on the road, and found some Indians encamped near it, and I tried to avoid them, but could not. An Indian came to me, who goes by the name of High-headed Jim, and who, I found, had been appointed to head a party sent to Autossee town, on the Tallapoosa, on a trip to Pensacola. he shook hands with me, and immediately began to tremble and jerk in every part of his frame, and the very calves of his legs were convulsed, and he would get entirely out of breath with the agitation. This practice was introduced in May or June last by "the Prophet Francis," who says that he was so instructed by the Spirit. High-headed Jim asked me what I meant to do. I said that I would sell my property, and buy ammunition from the governor; and join them. He then told me they were going down to Pensacola to get ammunition, and they had got a letter from a British general, which would enable them to receive ammunition from the governor; that it had been given to the Little Warrior, and was saved by his nephew when he was killed, and by him sent to Francis. High Head told me that, when they went back with their supply, another body of men would go down for another supply of ammunition; and that ten men were to go out of town, and they calculated on five horseloads for every town. He said they were to make a general attack on the American settlements; that the Indians on the waters of the Coosa, Tallapoosa, and Black Warrior were to attack the settlements on the Tombigby and Alabama, particularly the Tensas and Fork settlement that the Creek Indians bordering on the Cherokees were to attack the people of Tennessee, and that the Seminoles and Lower Creeks were to attack the Georgians; that the Choctas also had joined them and were to attack the Mississippi settlements; that the attack was to be made at the same time in all places, when they had become furnished with ammunition.

I found from my sister that they were treated very rigorously by the chiefs; and that many, especially the women, among them two daughters of the *late General McGillivray, who had been induced to join them in order to save their property, were very desirous of leaving them, but could not.*

I found from the talk of High Head that the war was to be against the whites, and not between the Indians themselves; that all they wanted was to kill those who had taken the talk of the white, viz: the Big Warrior, Alexander Curnells, Captain Isaac, William M'Intosh, the Mad Dragon's son, the Little Prince, Spoke Kange, and Tallasee Thicksico. They have destroyed a large quantity of my cattle, have burned my houses and my plantation, as well as those of James Curnells and Leonard M'Gee.

(Signed) Samuel (his S. M. mark) Moniac

Sworn to and subscribed before me, one of the United States judges for the Misssisppi Territory, this 2d day of August, 1813. Harry Toulmin

(A true copy) George T. Ross, Lieutenant-colonel of Volunteer

High Head Jim believed him and began to tell him of their plans to kill the peaceful chiefs, which included Big Warrior, Captain Isaacs, McIntosh and Mad Dragon's son. They believed that if the peaceful Creeks were deprived of their leaders, then those that remained would be compelled to join with the Red Sticks.

Once all the Creeks were united, they would begin the war by simultaneous attacks upon the white settlements. Having exterminated the whites upon their borders, they were to march in three columns against the people of Tennessee, Georgia, and Mississippi with assistance from the Choctaws and the Cherokees.

After High Head Jim and his party left, Moniac set out to inform the intended victims which enabled them to secure their safety. But the civil war increased in fury as hostile bands of Indians attacked the peaceful members of the Indian Nation, destroyed their houses, killed or drove off their cattle and stole their property.

In 1812, Congress responded to the violence taking place with the Native Americans and authorized the raising of a volunteer corps of fifty thousand men, to serve one year within two years after they were organized. General Andrew Jackson from Tennessee volunteered to lead men from Tennessee, and by November of 1812, a volunteer army of twenty-five hundred men joined him and were accepted as part of a national force.

The appearance of a British fleet off the Gulf coast awakened the American government to the danger in which Mobile lay, and on the 28th of June, 1813, Brigadier-General Ferdinand L. Claiborne, a distinguished soldier who had won a fine reputation in the Indian wars of the Northwest, was ordered, with what force he had, to march from the post of Baton Rouge to Fort Stoddard, a military station on the Mobile River, not far below the confluence of the Alabama and Tombigbee rivers.

"Upon receiving this order General Claiborne made application for the necessary funds and supplies, but the quartermaster could put no more than two hundred dollars into his army chest—a sum wholly inadequate to the purpose."

"Claiborne was not a man to permit small obstacles to interfere with affairs of importance. He borrowed the necessary funds upon his personal credit, giving a mortgage upon his property as security, and boldly set out with his little army. It is worth while to note in passing that, in consequence of the loss of vouchers for his expenditures upon the expedition, General Claiborne's patriotic act cost him the whole amount borrowed, his property being sold after his death, as we learn from a note in Pickett's *History of Alabama*, to satisfy the mortgage."

The Breaking Point

The hunting grounds of the Creeks once stretched across Georgia; but by treaties, first with Georgia and then with the United States, the bounds had been narrowed until in 1800 they were the Tennessee river, the western half of Georgia, and the Mississippi. Territory.

Benjamin Hawkins presided as agent for the United States over the Native Americans at the time. He had been appointed in 1796, and following the policy of the Government, he had taught the Native Americans how to plow and sow, raise crops, spin cotton, and even persuaded them to adopt a sort of national organization for the purpose of preserving peace and enforcing law.

Map of Indian Lands 1802 (Library of Congress)

In 1800, many of the Native Americans in what would become Alabama, dwelt in villages and owned farms, cattle, slaves, and knew the use of many implements of agriculture. Most of these villages, perhaps two thirds of them, belonged to the Upper Creeks, and were scattered along the banks of the Coosa and Tallapoosa rivers in the heart of what is now Alabama. The Lower Creek towns were on the Chattahoochee.

Hawkins had established a strong connection with the Native Americans and felt secure that they would never take up the tomahawk and give serious trouble. He knew the visit of Tecumseh had greatly excited the young warriors and that the prophets in the villages were busy teaching the young men in the villages war songs and dances of the Indians of the Great Lakes, but the old chiefs were peaceful and vigilant. No one was more surprised than Hawkins when he heard that the whole Upper Creek country was rising for war.

According to John Bach McMaster, the following series of events led to their war plans. The first began shortly after Tecumseh's visit.

In 1812, the Creek Nation dispatched a half dozen Indians on a mission to the Chickasaws. Little Warrior, a headman of a town called Wewocan, led the mission. Having delivered their "talk", they should have returned back to the Creek Nation in present day Alabama, but Little Warrior took them northward and joined Tecumseh at Malden. They were present at the massacre at the river Raisin, also known as the Battle of Frenchtown on January 18, 1813.

This massacre was a series of conflicts between the United States and a British and Native American alliance near the Rasin River in Frenchtown, Michgan Territory. Tecumseh commanded the native forces that fought in the battle, although he was not in Frenchtown at the time of the battle. This was the deadliest conflict recorded on Michigan soil, and the casualties included the highest number of Americans killed in a single battle during the War of 1812.

The group, exhilarated from the recent conflict, returned homeward and they carried "talks" from the British and the Shawnee, as well as a letter from a British officer at Malden to the Spanish officials at Pensacola. Crossing the present State of Illinois, Little Warrior and his band reached the Ohio River early in February and some seven miles above the mouth of the river they came upon the cabins of families of settlers.

Still excited from the success of their conflict at Raisin, the Native

Americans murdered these settlers on February 9, 1813. The band then crossed the Ohio, and hurried through the Chickasaw country, boasting of their deed as they went, and by the middle of March, they were once more on the Coosa River in Alabama.

Since Little Warrior had "talks" from the British, the chiefs all met with him at Tuckabatchie to hear them. The chiefs at the gathering were surprised to also receive a letter from the Indian Agent Benjamin Hawkins complaining of the murders of the settlers on the Ohio. As per the custom between the Americans and Native Americans at the time, Hawkins demanded the delivery of the seven murderers so they could be tried. The accused men immediately took off to the woods, but the chiefs declared them guilty, decreed death, and sent out two parties of warriors to carry out the sentence. Chief McIntosh commanded one party while Captain Isaacs led the other. Within a few days, all seven were dead.

Chief McIntosh (Alabama Department of Archives & History)

The incident and dire punishment caused much excitement in the Indian

Nation and war dances continued in earnest. The Nation was ripe for a civil war—a war of factions among themselves; it only needed a spark to create an explosion, and the spark was not long in coming. Outrages against friendly Native Americans and white settlers which were designed to force a war were committed. A United States mail-carrier was killed as he was traveling to Pensacola and the contents of his bags were stolen.

Prophets and orators in the Indian Nation denounced the "peacefuls," as they called the Creeks opposed to war. The old chiefs noticed the excitement and sent a message to the Alabamas, a small tribe living at the junction of the Coosa and Tallapoosa rivers who were greatly influenced by the prophets, particularly Red Eagle (also known as William Weatherford).

The old chiefs said, "We have heard much of what is going on among you, and how the Great Spirit comes in the sun and speaks to you. Let us see and hear some of these things, that we also may believe."

However, the Alabamas were in no state of mind to hear the message from the old chiefs. They killed the runner and sent his scalp about among their friends. Still the peaceful Native Americans remained true to their allegiance and fought their hostile brethren when the occasion required.

The killing of Little Warrior seemed to be the breaking point and the pent-up anger and excitement since Tecumseh's visit broke out. Every warrior who had borne a part in killing the murderers was driven from the country. Even the Tuckabatchee chiefs fled to Coweta and sought protection from Benjamin Hawkins.

About two thousand Native Americans, armed with red sticks and war clubs set out to kill all who had aided in putting Little Warrior and his band to death. They planned to destroy Tuckabatchee and Coweta, march against the whites, and not leave one white man or friendly Native American living between the Chattahoochee and the sea. The warriors were called 'Red Sticks' because of the red sticks they carried, and along with bows, arrow, and the magic of the prophets, they were determined that they would be successful.

Revenge

The Battle Of Burnt Corn

When Little Warrior was killed, the letter he was carrying from the British at Malden to the Spaniards at Pensacola which requested that the Spanish help the Creeks by supplying them with arms, had fallen into the hands of the half-Creek Indian named Peter McQueen. In July 1813, Peter McQueen, High Head Jim and the Prophet Francis, all Red Sticks, had collected a large amount of plunder and four hundred dollars in their descents upon the homes of peaceful Native American plantations and they sought a market for their booty.

McQueen led around three hundred warriors as he set out with the letter, and plunder for Pensacola. While en-route to Pensacola the Red Sticks continued to burn villages and murder peaceful Indians they found on the way. Though they had Creek ancestry, the plantations of Sam Moniac and James Cornells were burned and James Cornell's wife was kidnapped. When the Native Americans arrived in Pensacola, the Spanish Governor was so fearful of the Indians that he gave them everything they needed by way of trade. Thus, the Red Sticks acquired needed guns, powder, and ball.

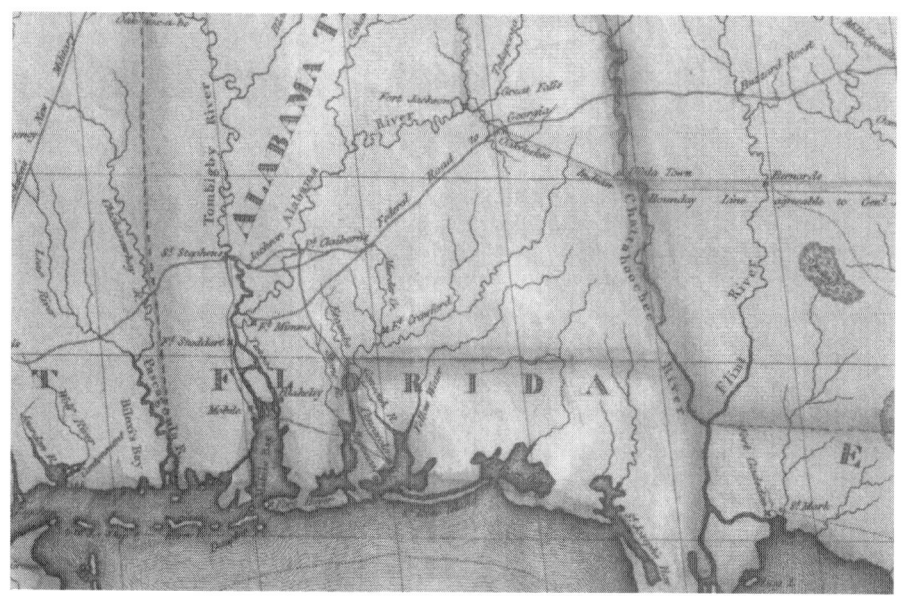

Map showing location of Tombigbee River and Pensacola, Florida (Library of Congress)

News of McQueen's visit to Pensacola spread rapidly among the Americans settled around Mobile, Alabama. At the same time, the British were threatening to descend upon them. It appeared that the Red Sticks were only delaying all out war until the British, who were their allies, could arrive on the coast and attack the militia of the Tensaw and Tombigbee settlements. Through spies, it was also learned that the Indians had procured 300 pounds of powder and a quantity of lead from the Governor Manique of Pensacola. It appeared that the small white settlements around Mobile would be easily exterminated by the combined forces of the British and Red Sticks.

The Americans were determined to cut the marauding Red Sticks off as they traveled home from Pensacola. If they could crush them, they believed that the great body of Creeks would think twice before deciding to make war. A summons was sent out for volunteers and about two hundred men, some white, some half-Indian, and a few friendly Native Americans, responded to the call. Captain Samuel Dale, better known in history as Sam Dale, the hero of the canoe fight was among them.

Commanded by Colonel Caller, who was the senior militia officer of Washington County in the Mississippi Territory, the little army which probably had about one officer to every two men, set out to meet Peter McQueen and his force as they returned from Pensacola. On July 25th the army crossed the Tombigbee and on the night of July 26th, he camped near the town of Bellville, Alabama.

On July 27th, 1813, advance scouts reported that McQueen's men were encamped nearby on Burnt Corn Creek "enjoying a noon-day meal at a bend in the creek, called the Old Wolf Path," and they seemed to be unaware of the approaching militia. Captain Caller formed his men in line and cautiously advanced through the reeds until the camp lay just below, and then with a yell, the men dashed forward in a charge. The surprised Red Sticks gave some resistance, but soon abandoned their camp, and left their rich stores of ammunition and food. They fled to Burnt Corn Creek that encircled the camp and waited.

Captain Samuel Dale, Captain Dixon Bailey, and Captain Benjamin Smoot along with eighty men attempted to pursue the Indians in order to crush them entirely. The majority of the Americans remained behind. When the Red Sticks ran, they left behind their pack-horses loaded with goods. The officers and men of the main body evidently decided that their work was done when they rousted the Red Sticks, and instead of joining in the pursuit, they broke their ranks, threw down their arms, and busied themselves securing the plunder.

Seeing only a small number of men pursuing them, Peter McQueen rallied his men and gave the group a battle. The brave but untrained, inexperienced and outnumbered men under the command of Captain Dale, Captain Smoot, and Captain Bailey were forced back.

Peter McQueen took the advantage and advanced. The men of the main body who were still plundering the camp, had abandoned their arms, and "were in no condition to fight and seeing the advance companies retreating with the yelling Indians at their heels, they fled precipitately." Having left their horses unattended, the militia members fled on foot or mounted the nearest horses, which even included the pack animals.

Caller, Dale, Bailey, and Smoot tried to rally the men, but succeeded only in getting a few men into line. This small force, commanded by their brave officers, made a desperate stand, and finally brought the advancing savages to a halt. Dale was severely wounded, but he fought on in spite of his suffering and his weakness.

Finally, seeing that they were over-matched and that their comrades had abandoned them to their fate, the little band retreated, fighting as they went, until at last the Indians gave up the pursuit. Some of the Americans went home, others became "lost and were found, nearly dead with fatigue and starvation, about a fortnight later."

Caller and one of his officers became lost in the swampy woods and were rescued about two weeks later, malnourished and delirious. Alexandre Hollinger, son of Adam Hollinger and Marie Joseph Juzan was among the wounded at Burnt Corn.

George C. Eggleston states in his book, *Red Eagle; or, Wars with the Indians of Alabama,*

"Thus ended the battle of Burnt Corn. It was lost to the white men solely by the misconduct of officers and men, but that misconduct was the result of inexperience and a want of discipline, not of cowardice or any lack of manhood."

The militia's casualties included two dead and ten to fifteen wounded while the Red Sticks were reported to have lost ten men. The militia managed to take much of the shot and powder from the Creeks.

"Reportedly, all of the men who took part in the battle immediately mustered out of the militia, and those who were identified as participants were subjected to public ridicule for many years afterward."

On the 30th day of July, 1813, General Claiborne arrived at Fort Stoddard (Stodhert) with his army of seven hundred men and immediately assessed the situation. He distributed his forces and the volunteers under his command to the various stockade posts in such a way as to give the best protection he could to every part of the country. General Claiborne sent Major Beasley with one hundred and seventy-five men with seventy militiamen already there, which swelled the force at that post to two hundred and forty-five fighting men.

Red Eagle led his people to retaliate for the killing of Native Americans at the battle of Burnt Corn. The Native American raid on Fort Mims took place August 30, 1813 and triggered the outbreak of the Creek War.

Terrified Settlers Abandon Farms

After the Burnt Corn battle, McQueen planned to attack Hawkins at the Indian Agency at Coweta, but the families of the Red Sticks who were killed and wounded at Burnt Corn cried out for vengeance, so McQueen and around one thousand warriors of the Upper Creek towns set out in search of the men who had attacked them at Burnt Corn.

Terrified settlers heard of the battle at Burnt Corn and abandoned their homes and farms as they fled for shelter of well-known wealthy men in their communities and they began to fortify themselves. Soon the whole country between Alabama and the Tombigbee rivers was dotted with rude defenses where several hundred men, women, children, and slaves gathered. "They were called forts; but were in reality stockades hastily put up around a house, whose size, strength, and location made it capable of being defended." There were more than a twenty of these hastily built forts in different parts of settlements, each taking its name from the owner of the place fortified.

One such fort was on Samuel Mims plantation which was located on an old bend of the Alabama River. The bend had been cut off from the main river and was now a small lake on his property. Mim's house was only a large frame building around which the people had built a stockade in the form of a square and enclosed about an acre of land.

The fort was made with timbers set on end in the ground as close together as possible, forming a close and high wall. The wall was pierced with five hundred port-holes for the use of riflemen. Two heavy gates were provided to gain entrance. There was a partially built block-house at one corner.

The troops at Fort Mims consisted of militia and volunteers sent by General Ferdinand Leigh Claiborne from Baton Rouge led by Major Beasley. Believing the post to be strong enough to spare a part of the force under his command, Major Beasley sent detachments to various other weaker posts. Tensaw settlers poured into the stockade until by

August there were around five hundred and fifty-three men, women, children, slaves, friendly Native Americans, troops, and officers in the fort.

The lives of all these people were committed to the keeping of Major Beasley. From the first, alarms of an impending attack occurred frequently which Beasley reported to General Claiborne. In response, General Claiborne gave a general order for Major Beasley to strengthen the fort, use caution in conducting affairs and neglect no means of making the fort secure. He directed Major Beasley to build two additional block-houses, but Major Beasley only partially built one.

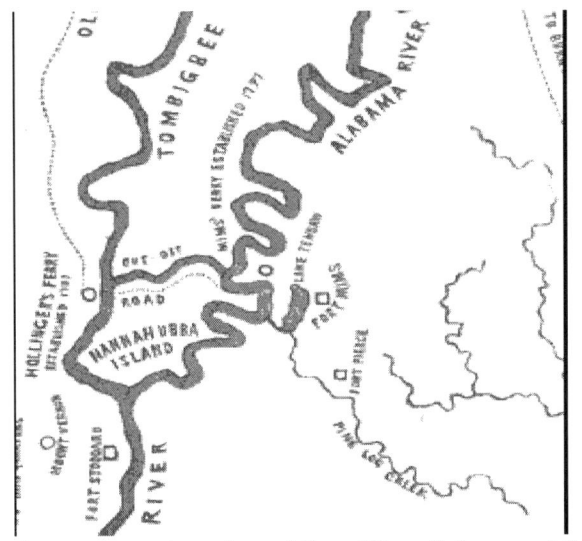

Portion of map shows location of Fort Mims (Library of Congress)

When reports reached the Red Sticks that two of the men who attacked the Red Sticks, Dixon Bailey and Daniel Beasley, were at Fort Mims, their expedition set out for this place.

Lucy Cornell, Red Eagle's sweetheart and her family had taken refuge in Fort Mims at the time, and when Red Eagle learned of this, it is believed that his love for Lucy prompted him to give a secret warning to her father of the impending attack on Fort Mims because Cornell left the fort prior to the attack. Although Cornell remained with the whites and fought with them in the war, he allowed Red Eagle to carry off his daughter to the Creek Nation.

About this time, Chief Red Eagle, who was still reluctant to fight in a war, sought the advice of his brother, Jack Weatherford, and his half-brother, David Tate (Tait) who had homes on Little River. They advised him to secretly remove his family, slaves, and much of his live-stock to their plantations which lay within the friendly district, and quit the Nation and not take part in the impending war. Red Eagle decided to act on their advice, but when he returned to his plantation, he found he was too late. Some Red Sticks, realized that their chief had many reasons for abandoning their cause, and had seized his children and slaves as hostages for his fidelity. They threatened to kill his children if he should falter. There was nothing left for him to do but yield to his fate and lead the Red Sticks into battle.

Red Eagle collected his men and began moving secretly down the river. When he reached Zachariah McGirth's plantation on the Alabama River in the neighborhood of Claiborne, it appeared to many that he planned to attack Fort Glass and Fort Sinquefield in what is now Clarke County, Alabama.

Meanwhile, General Claiborne wrote to his commanding general of his plans to take the offensive against the Native Americans in the following letter of the 2nd of August, 1813:

"If you will authorize my entering the Creek nation, I will do so in ten days after the junction of the Seventh Regiment, and if I am not disappointed, will give to our frontiers peace, and to the government any portion of the Creek country they please. Some force ought to enter the nation before they systematize and are fully prepared for war. With one thousand men and your authority to march immediately, I pledge myself to burn any town in the Creek nation. Three months hence it might be difficult for three thousand to effect what can be done with a third of the number at present. They gain strength, and their munitions of war enlarge every day."

However, this request was not allowed because the Creeks had not yet openly attacked the white settlements beyond their border, and until they did so the commanding general had no authority to permit his troops to invade the Creek Nation.

General Claiborne visited all the forts, inspected them, and gave minute and careful instructions to strengthen them and warned the militiamen not to be lulled into a dangerous feeling of security by delay and by repeated false alarms. Once he delivered his orders, General Claiborne went to the most exposed point, a small fort about sixty miles further into the Native American country, believing that Red Eagle would make his first attack there.

Massacres

Surprise Attack

The people in Fort Mims were singing, playing games, and going about their daily routines, and the soldiers were completely off their guard on the 30th of August, 1813. The drum announced dinner at noon and this was the signal Red Eagle was waiting for.

As the people gathered for their noon meal, Red Eagle advanced his line slowly, determined to take the fort by complete surprise. Amazingly, no one noticed their approach until the Red Sticks were within thirty yards of the open gate. At that instant a few white men saw them and rushed to close the open gate, but as they pushed against the heavy gate, the accumulated sand at its base prevented it from moving. It was too late—the Red Sticks rushed in and were within the outer lines of the the defensive works.

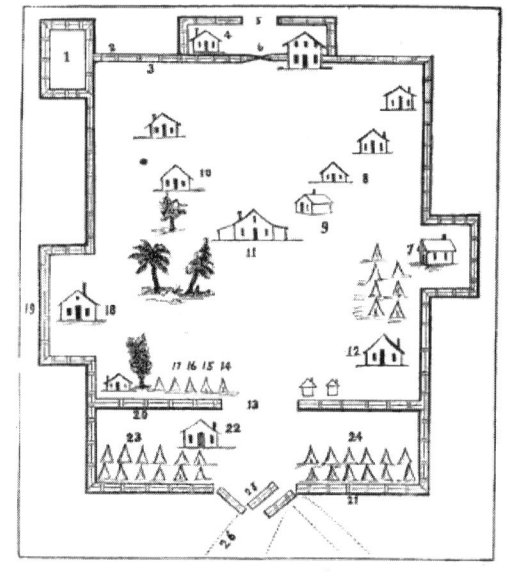

FORT MIMS (INTERIOR).

Layout of Fort Mims (Library of Congress)

The partially finished second line of picketing provided some defensive work where the whites made an attempt to fight off their foes. Major Beasley was the one of the first to confront the enemy and one of the first to fall, mortally wounded. He continued to command until the last breath left his body.

The Red Sticks fought not to conquer, but instead to kill the whites. Everyone, all the men as well as the women and children found themselves in hand-to-hand conflict with knives, tomahawks and clubbed guns.

When the first Creek prophets fell, some of the Red Sticks hesitated for a moment because they had been told that the prophets bodies were invulnerable and would receive no harm, but then the fight immediately continued with even more vengeance in revenge for their deaths. Everyone within the fort who could shoot a gun, or strike a blow with axe or club was engaged in the fight for their lives.

Captain Middleton had charge of the eastern side, but soon fell at his post while Captain Jack fought desperately on the southern face and Lieutenant Randon on the west. Captain Dixon Bailey, who had been at the battle of Burnt Corn, fought on the northern face. It is believed that the fighting white men were outnumbered at least three to one and the Native Americans steadily gained ground.

Two brothers of Captain Dixon Bailey, James and Daniel Bailey, went with some men into Mim's house and pierced the roof with port-holes to fire on the Red Stick warriors. Burning arrows were fired into the shingles of the house setting it on fire forcing them to withdraw.

Little by little the fort yielded. The remaining whites, mostly women and children, retreated to the only remaining building, a small enclosure around the loom house called the bastion. Soon the bastion was so full of people that there was scarcely room for anyone to move. The Red Sticks danced, shrieked and howled outside the small building, while the people inside could do nothing but wring their hands and commit themselves to heaven while awaiting certain death.

"Red Eagle was a soldier, not a butcher; and now that his victory was secure he sought to stop the bloodshed and spare the lives of the helpless people who remained; he called upon his warriors to desist and to receive the survivors as prisoners, but the yelling savages would not listen to him."

His followers remembered that he had tried to withdraw from the war, and with loud shrieks of anger, they turned on him and threatened to put him to death if he should further plead for mercy. "He could do nothing but submit, and turn away in horror from the sight of the brutal slaughter which he had made possible. It as reported that he mounted his horse and rode away, resolved to have at least no personal share in the horrible butchery."

A few people made a hole in the outer picketing and made a dash for life. Of these about twenty escaped in different directions, and in one way or another managed to reach other forts. All the rest of the people were killed.

The known persons who escaped by flight were Dr. Thomas G. Homes, a black woman named Hester, a friendly Indian names Socca, Lieutenant Peter Randon, Josiah Fletcher, Sergeant Matthews, Martin Rigdon, Samuel Smith, a half-Indian, Joseph Perry, Jesse Steadham, Edward Steadham, John Horen, Lieutenant W. R. Chambers, two men named Mourrice and Jones, and a few others.

The battle lasted for five hours without cessation. On September 9th, when an officer sent by General Claiborne with a strong detachment to bury the dead reached Fort Mims he found a piece of the stockade and the unfinished block-house alone remaining. The land about the fort was Native Americans, women, and children, all scalped and mutilated.

Survivor Stories From Fort Mims

Dr. Thomas G. Holmes

Dr. Thomas G. Holmes was a survivor who had cut the hole through the picket fences where many people made their escape. Anticipating a break through the pickets, several Red Sticks placed themselves in position along the fence to block their attempt. It was amazing that anyone escaped. Dr. Holmes' clothes were riddled with bullets as he ran, but he made it to the thick woods unhurt and concealed himself in a hole made by a large uprooted tree. There he remained until nightfall even though the Red Sticks beat the bushes surrounding Fort Mims in every direction searching for anyone who might have escaped.

At night, the light from burning buildings prevented him from leaving immediately. However, once the Red Sticks fell asleep around their campfires, he made his way out of the woods. Since he could not swim, he was unable to cross the river so he wandered in the swamp for five days, living on roots and other things until he reached a home of a friend. No one was at the house. Dr. Holmes fired his gun in the hopes of attracting attention in case they were elsewhere on the farm. However, the unexpected gunfire alarmed the family and they fled to the river where they remained for two days. Left alone and famished, Holmes went to the chicken pen, caught a chicken, and ate it raw. Finally, the owners of the house returned, and he was taken to a place of safety.[4]

Lieutenant Chambliss

Lieutenant Chambliss was severely wounded twice as he fled. He concealed himself in a heap of logs in the woods. Around dark some roving Red Sticks set fire to the log heap. The fire ate away at the log pile, but Lieutenant Chambliss remained still. Though he risked being burned alive, he knew he faced certain death if he fled with the Red Sticks so near.

Finally, the Red Sticks lit their pipes and walked away. Lieutenant Chambliss silently crept away from the burning pile and concealed

---

[4] Dr. Holmes related his experiences to Historian Albert J. Pickett many years later.

himself some distance from their camp. He wandered in the woods for several days, wounded and famished until at last he reached the safety of the settlement at Mount Vernon.

Zachariah McGirth

Zachariah McGirth resided at Fort Mims with his half-Indian wife and their children. Accompanied by a few of his slaves, Zachariah left by boat on the morning of the massacre to check on his plantation at a point high up on the Alabama River. He was some distance from Fort Mims when he heard the gunfire from the massacre taking place. Zachariah had left his wife and children at the fort so he immediately turned back.

When he drew near and saw what was taking place in the fort, he and his slaves hid in the woods, where they watched and waited at a safe distance. After the sound of musketry died away, Zachariah was desperate to learn what happened to his family. He told his slaves to remain hidden in the woods, then he boldly entered the scene of the slaughter.

Zachariah found no Red Sticks inside the fort so he went back and summoned his slaves and they began a painstaking for his wife and children among the dead, but they were not found. Zacahariah assumed that they were burned in one of the buildings.

But his story does not end there. McGirth's wife and children were spared because of a kindness by his wife. It seems that a young warrior among the Red Sticks had been an orphan and hungry when he was a young boy, when McGirth's wife found him and tenderly cared for him. During the horrible fight at Fort Mims, this young warrior happened to recognize the woman who had befriended him in his time of need. And in order to save her and her children, he told his comrades that he wished to make them his slaves. Under this pretense he carried them back to his home in the Creek Nation.

Of course, McGirth knew nothing of this, and after the massacre, he became entirely reckless and continually risked his life in dangerous situations. It was said that he didn't care whether he lived or died. He was only bent on the destruction of all Creeks who had killed his wife and children.

Zachariah went on to became the most daring scout and express rider in the American service. Then one day, several months after the massacres at Fort Mims, McGirth was in Mobile when someone came to him with a message. A party of poor Indians had made their way down the river from the hostile country and wished to see him. Answering the summons, Zachariah was ushered into the presence of his wife and seven children. It was as if they had suddenly arisen from the dead.

Kimball James Massacre & Fort Sinquefield

On August 31, 1813, the Tory Creek Nah-he, a friendly Creek, returned to Fort Madison to report of the massacre at Fort Mims. He also informed the officers in charge that a large force of hostile Creeks led by Prophet Josiah Francis were gathered on the Alabama River. Nah-he scouted that evening while the men in Fort Madison made preparations for an attack.

Ransom Kimball and Abner James had taken shelter at Fort Sinquefield in August, 1813 with many other settlers and friendly Native Americans, but there were so many people in the stockade that they decided to take their chances and returned to the Kimball's plantation in Bassett's Creek Valley which was about two miles from Fort Sinquefield.

On the evening of August 31, 1813, Mary James, the daughter of Abner James was up late caring for a sick family member when she heard the dogs barking outside. She quickly blew out the candles and was alarmed when she heard the sound of running feet. Still, the two families decided to remain at the plantation house.

The next day Ransom Kimball was away from the house when the families realized that the house was surrounded by Red Sticks. Hostile Creeks led by the Prophet Francis attacked the plantation. Twelve of the seventeen members of the Kimball and James families were killed. A few family members escaped, including Mrs. Sarah Merrill, a daughter of Abner James.

As she ran with her infant son, she was struck down, scalped and left for dead. She lay senseless for many hours, but was revived by a falling rain.

Though severely injured herself, she sought for her infant among the dead bodies and was overjoyed to find her child still alive. She immediately made her way to the fort with her child, but being nearly half-dead herself, she found her strength failing. She hid her infant and crawled the remaining distance to Fort Sinquefield where she entreated someone to rescue her child. Both Mrs. Merrill and her infant eventually recovered.[5]

During his scouting, Nah-he learned about the atrocities that had taken place at the Kimball plantation and relayed the news to Captain Joseph Carson. Eleven men under the command of Lieutenant James Bailey had been sent to Fort Sinquefield to assist in the burials of the Fort Mims dead. On September 2, 1813, Lieutenant James Bailey led the party of eleven well-armed men which included John Woods, Isaac Hayden and James Smith to retrieve the bodies of the dead from the Kimball plantation.

Around 11:00 am the same day, during the burial ceremony of the Kimballs about 70 yards southeast of the fort, one hundred Red Sticks were seen stealthily approaching the stockade.

Some women had taken the opportunity to do some washing at a spring down hill from the burial party. One woman was an African American woman, Sarah Phillips, the wife of Charles Phillips, Jr. There was a small guard detail with them as they carried their buckets and walked down to the spring. The guards did not follow the women all the way to the spring. Instead, they stood in the shade of a tree, talking.

---

5 Mrs. Merrill's husband was away serving as a volunteer under General Caliborne around the same time of Mrs. Merrill's near-death experience when he received word of her death. Tragically, Mrs. Merrill also received word that he was terribly wounded and left for dead on the battlefield. However in a strange coincidence, Merrill had recovered from consciousness after his comrades left the field and he fell in with some Tennessee volunteers. He was sent with their wounded to Tennessee, where, after a long period of recuperation, he was finally restored to health. Several years passed and Mrs. Merrill, believing her husband dead, married again. She was living with her second husband and additional children when one evening a family from Tennessee, who was moving to Texas, stopped at her house. As was the custom, she offered them accommodations for the night, and they had scarcely settled in as guests before the head of the family and the wife of the host recognized each other. One was Merrill and the other was his wife, and both had married again. After some discussion, it was decided that as each had acted in good faith, and both the families were happy, then it would be best to let matters stand. Mrs. Merrill lived in Clarke County, Alabama until her death in 1869.

Charles Phillips, Sr. and Isham Kimball were sitting by the gate talking about the massacres when Phillips glanced south and saw a flock of turkeys coming toward the fort. He pointed to them, and Kimball realized they weren't turkeys. They were Red Sticks!

The alarm was given, all the Native Americans rose and ran full speed to cut off the burial party. The burial party and the women rushed for the gate. Unable to reach the burial party, the Red Sticks saw the terrified women running uphill from the spring and set out after them.

Isaac Hayden, who often hunted with his dogs, leaped on a horse, and then he called forth the dogs, about 60 in all that were within fort, and set the yelping pack upon the Indians. This delay enabled the women, with the exception of Mrs. Sarah Phillips, to reach the fort in safety. Mrs. Phillips, who was pregnant and unable to move quickly was overtaken and killed. One young girl, Winnie Odum, collapsed outside the fort and a soldier reached out and grabbed her by the hair and pulled her inside.

Charles Phillips, Jr. tried to run out of the fort to kill the Indians that had killed his wife, but he was held back by friends.

Hayden's horse was shot in the neck and killed under him as he made a mad dash back to the fort and the gate was closed.[6] It was discovered that five bullets had passed through his clothes once he was inside the fort, but he was unharmed.

The Red Sticks surrounded the stockade. James Short fired from inside the fort but his gun sputtered from old powder. The Red Sticks thought the whites were running out of powder and shouted in victory. Prophet Francis waved a cow tail and yelled to his warriors to attack. Shots rang out from inside the fort and Prophet Francis was immediately shot dead. The fight was on!

Women and children screamed as the men moved to the lower story of the block-house. The women sprang into action and stayed busy molding

---

6   The horse recovered but all the dogs were lost in the woods.

bullets while James Smith, Stephen Lacey and others in the upper story of the block-house fired a continuous barrage of gunshots at the Indians. During the melee, Mrs. Lacey and Mrs. Thomas Phillips came up to the 2nd story to deliver some bullets and at that same moment, her husband, Stephen Lacey, was shot and fell mortally wounded at the feet of his wife. Mrs. Lacey was cautioned to keep quiet and though overwhelmed by grief, she did not cry out. A ten-year old, James Dubose, was also shot and slightly wounded.

The attack lasted only two hours. John Woods fired the final shot and the Red Sticks finally retreated, but took all the horses they could find near the fort.

That evening, Charles Phillips, Jr. went out to recover his wife's body. She and Lacey were buried that same night.

Some men followed the Red Stick's trail, but later returned to Fort Sinquefield. It was decided that they should abandon the fort and move to nearby Fort Madison for safety. The fearful residents moved in small groups. It was told that one man, "George Bunch was so frightened, that he left his poor wife and children and was the first to arrive at Madison. Mrs. Bunch put her most prized belongings into a sack and set out for safety with her two young children; moving slowly, and it took them all the terrifying night to get to Madison. They were the last to arrive and, safe at last, Mrs. Bunch fell in a swoon into the ministering hands of her friends and neighbors."

Danger continued at Fort Madison. Four men went outside the fort to some nearby fields to collect some green vegetables and while gathering food, they were attacked by the Red Sticks and two of them were shot. After their attack, Colonel Carson, who was commanding Fort Madison was satisfied that Red Eagle planned to attack Fort Madison next so he decided to call upon General Claiborne for assistance. Jeremiah Austill volunteered on the dangerous mission to take the dispatch to Colonel Claiborne. He traveled all night and reached Colonel Claiborne the following morning.

Colonel Claiborne commended Austill's courage, but had no troops to spare so Austill returned to Fort Madison with the message that they should abandon the Fort and retire with his garrison and inmates to Fort Stephen's which was a more strategic post.

Many at Fort Madison refused to abandon it. Shortly after Austill arrived, another order from Claiborne arrived with the message "not to abandon the fort unless it is clear that you cannot hold it."

Chaos and Panic

Pushmataha Offers Assistance

After Fort Mims was destroyed, the Red Sticks were in a high state of excitement which spread over the land. They burned homes, destroyed crops, and murdered every white man with whom they came in contact. Panic seized the whole population of the Mississippi Territory. Settlers abandoned their homesteads and fled to the confines of the forts. Three hundred and ninety people were housed at Fort Huron, at Fort Rankin were five hundred and thirty, and at Fort St. Stephens were five hundred settlers. Two forts at Mount Vernon were packed with refuges. Urgent requests for help were sent to the Governors of Louisiana, of Georgia, and of Tennessee.

The Creeks were divided into two parties after Fort Mims, the friendly Native Americans and the Red Sticks, but the war party prevailed while the other looked to the United States for protection. There was great anxiety that the Chickasaws and Choctaws would be drawn into the conflict as allies.

In southern part of what would become Alabama, settlers had quickly armed themselves. A small group of twenty-five rural pioneer Alabama militia were scouting the sparsely settled area of Wood's Bluff and Bashi Creek in the fall of 1813 when they were ambushed by Red Sticks. They were led by Colonel William McGrew who had taken part in the Battle of Burnt Corn, to a stream called Bashi Creek which flowed into the Tombigbee River a mile or two north of Wood's Bluff when they suddenly found themselves among concealed Creek warriors.

A turkey tail was raised above a log by one of the concealed Creek which was the signal for attack and the Native Americans began firing. Colonel McGrew was killed along with Private Edmund Miles, Jesse Griffin, and Captain William Bradbury. David Griffin (twin of Jesse Griffin) was reported missing and presumed dead; his body was never found. Days later, a military column passed by and buried the deceased pioneer militia members with military honors.

The few troops under Claiborne's command, together with the militia of the country, were barely sufficient to hold the forts, and even this inadequate force was liable at any time to be reduced by the withdrawal of the soldiers to assist in repelling an attack of the British whose fleet now constantly threatened the coast; and if the forces of the Choctaws and Chickasaws should be added to Red Eagle's strength, the plight of the whites would indeed be profound.

About this time a Choctaw chief of influence with his people, by name Pushmatahaw, arrived at St. Stephen's, and declared that he could induce a considerable number of the Choctaw warriors to enlist in the American service if permission was given to recruit among them.

Choctaw Chief Pushmatahaw (Alabama Department of Archives and History)

Eagerly grasping at this hope, Colonel George S. Gaines went with the chief to Mobile to secure the desired authority from General Flournoy, who was now in command of the southwestern department.

That officer, for some reason which is not apparent, declined to accept the services of the Choctaws and Colonel Gaines and his companion returned with heavy hearts to St. Stephen's with the sad news. However, before Pushmatahaw had taken his departure, a courier from General Flournoy arrived with the order for Colonel Gaines to accept the friendly chief's offer of assistance and to accompany him to the Choctaw Nation to enlist the men.

With a single white companion, Colonel Gaines went with Pushmatahaw to the nation where, gathering the Choctaws into a council, the chief made them a speech, saying that Tecumseh, who had suggested this war, was a bad man. He added:

"He came through our country, but did not turn our heads. He went among the Muscogees, and got many of them to join him. You know the Tensaw people. They were our friends. They played ball with us. They sheltered and fed us when we went to Pensacola. Where are they now? Their bodies are rotting at Sam Mims's place. The people at St. Stephen's are also our friends. The Muscogees intend to kill them too. They want soldiers to defend them. You can all do as you please. You are free men. I dictate to none of you; but I shall join the St. Stephen's people. If you have a mind to follow me, I will lead you to glory and to victory."

Pushmatahaw finished this speech with his drawn sword in his hand. When he paused, one of the silent warriors stood up and, striking his breast with his open palm, after the manner of the Choctaws on specially solemn occasions, said, " I am a man; I will follow you." Whereupon his fellows imitated his example, and thus a considerable force of men, who might have been added to Weatherford's strength but for the friendliness of Pushmatahaw, became active friends of the whites.

During this time before railroads and steamboats, it took more than a month for the swiftest messenger from Alabama to reach New York. In this perilous situation of affairs it was useless for General Claiborne, or his superior officer, General Flournoy, to appeal to the government at Washington for aid. Even if the troops of the Government had not been fully occupied already in other parts of the country, the distance was so great that any assistance which the general government might be able to render must of necessity come too late to be of any avail. It would take a month for the messenger asking for help to reach Washington, another month for a force to be gathered, and perhaps two months more for it to reach the exposed point. Three or four months at least, and probably a greater time, must pass before help could come from that quarter, and it might as well have taken a hundred years so far as all practical purposes were concerned.

Therefore, the only sure resource was an appeal to the people of the surrounding states. Urgent requests for help were sent to the Governors in South Carolina, Georgia, and Tennessee, carrying dispatches which simply set forth the facts and the danger. The response was quick and generous. Georgians and South Carolinians began at once to organize forces, which soon afterward invaded the Creek country. But the most efficient aid was to come from Tennessee, a state which had already shown itself quick to answer to every demand made upon it.

Tennessee had furnished its full quotas of men to the national army; and in less than a year it had sent a full division of volunteers under Jackson to reinforce the army at New Orleans. This division had been ordered to disband while at Natchez, when they were without money or provisions with which to reach their homes, but Jackson had resolutely disobeyed the order, and instead of disbanding his division had marched it back to Tennessee in a body.

Meanwhile, the Red Sticks war party had gathered a formidable body in early October, and were said to have been directing their course towards the frontiers of Tennessee.

Tennessee Responds To The Call

On the 18th day of September, the people of Nashville assembled in a public meeting to consider the news which had just been received.

There was unfortunately no law of the State under which anybody was authorized to call out the needed men, and although Governor Blount was ready to approve and actively to encourage the gathering of Tennessee's strength and its use in this way, he had no legal authority to promise pay or support to the troops. This defect was repaired by the Legislature within a week. That body passed a bill authorizing the governor to enlist three thousand five hundred men for this service, voting three hundred thousand dollars for expenses, and pledging the State to support and pay the men, if the general government should refuse or neglect to accept the force as a part of its volunteer army. The governor of Tennessee issued an order to General Andrew Jackson to call out 2000 militia immediately and rendezvous at Fayetteville.

At the time, Andrew Jackson was still recuperating from a wound received in a street brawl with Thomas Hart Benton and was confined to his home with a fractured arm. Notwithstanding, he obeyed the call. On the 26th day of September, just one week after the Sunday when the public meeting had been held, he ordered Colonel Coffee with his cavalry of five hundred strong and his mounted rifleman to proceed to Huntsville in order to cover the frontier until the infantry could catch up.

The men assembled on October 4th, but Jackson did not attend due to his injury. In his stead, he sent his aid, Major Reid. The Ten Islands is believed to be their place of assemblage. Reid established strict regulations within camp. Friendly Creeks acted in unison with the infantry and served as spies in conveying information concerning the Red Sticks.

Coffee received volunteers at every cross-road, and by the time he arrived at Fayetteville, the appointed place of rendezvous, his five hundred men had increased to one thousand three hundred.

By the second week in October, 1813, twenty-five hundred infantry and a thousand cavalry crossed the Tennessee River and camped in the present state of Alabama. Along with them were David Crockett and a young ensign named Samuel Houston. After a time, the troops advanced to Thompson's Creek to await the arrival of much needed supplies ordered from East Tennessee.

Andrew Jackson (Alabama Department of Archives and History)

Jackson had to be helped on his horse when he set out to join the army he had raised so speedily. His arm was still encased in the surgeon's wrappings, and carried in a sling. He could put but one arm into his coat-sleeve, and he was so weak that it was with difficulty that he could ride at all; but there was that in his composition which had already gained for him his nickname, "Old Hickory;" it was the tough hickory of his nature which supplied the place of physical strength, and enabled him to march.

On evening of the 11th of October, Jackson arrived at Huntsville, Alabama. He marched the troops to Ditto's landing to await the arrival of provisions for the army. He wanted to advance but without provisions he could not move forward. He ordered Coffee with his cavalry to scour the country for supplies. Having secured his men, Jackson's next care was to convert them as rapidly as possible into soldiers, and accordingly his next appeal was directed to this end.

Around the middle of October, Jackson directed General John Coffee with his eight hundred Tennessee cavalrymen to head for the Native American town of Black Warrior and burn it to the ground. In this body was the celebrated David Crockett who described the event in his a biography he wrote and published in 1843. He wrote as follows:

"We pushed on till we got to what was called the Black Warrior's Town, which stood near the very spot where Tuscaloosa now stands, which is the seat of Government for the State of Alabama. The Indian town was a large one; but when we arrived we found that the Indians had all left it. There was a large field of corn standing out, and a pretty good supply in some of the cribs. There was also a fine quantity of dried beans, which was very acceptable to us; and without delay we secured them as well as the corn, and then burned the town to ashes. After that we left the place. In the field where we gathered the corn we saw plenty of fresh Indian tracks and we had no doubt they had been scared off by our arrival. That evening we got as far back as the encampment we made the night before we reached Black Warrior's Town, which we had just destroyed."

Andrew Jackson's troops set out through one hundred and sixty miles of wilderness toward Hickory Ground at the junction of the Coosa and Tallapoosa Rivers where many of the fighting Creeks lived.

Jackson sent his mounted men forward to forage and "fairly dragged his troops over the roughest of countries to a spot where the Tennessee makes its great south bend, and there, in a mountain pass, established Fort Deposit at Thompson's Creek. This done, he turned southward into the wilderness, determined to seek food as he went."

The state of affairs when Jackson left Fort Deposit, on Thompson's Creek, where he tarried but a single day, may be inferred from a letter written by Major John Reid, of the general's staff. The whole letter is printed in

Parton's Life of Jackson.

"At this place we have remained a day for the purpose of establishing a depot for provisions; but where these provisions are to come from God Almighty only knows. We had expected supplies from East Tennessee, but they have not arrived, and I am fearful never will. I speak seriously when I declare I expect we shall soon have to eat our horses, and perhaps this is the best use we can put a great many of them to."

On the 25th of October Jackson and his men set out and within ten days they had reached the head waters of the Coosa. General Jackson learned that the enemy was posted in force at the Creek town of Tallaseehatchee at the beginning of November, a distance of about thirteen miles on the south banks of the Coosa. General Coffee with a body of nine hundred men was sent to dislodge them while Jackson began the erection of Fort Strother.

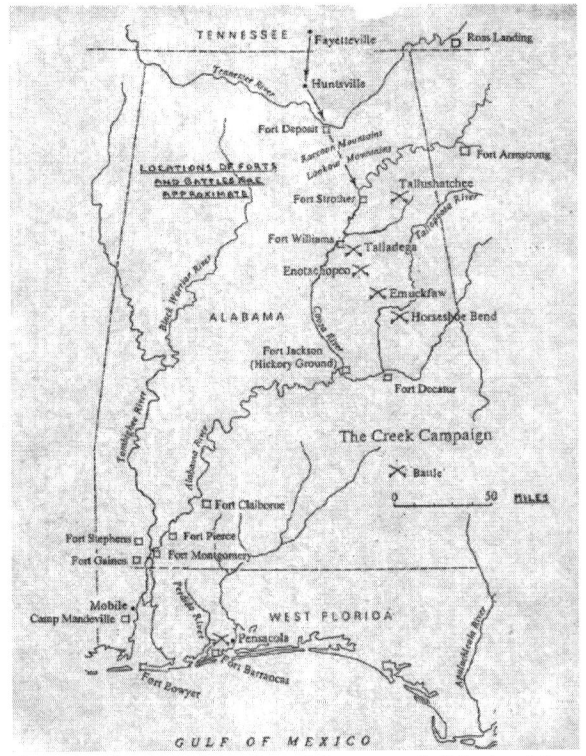

Many of the forts in the Creek Indian War are visible in this map (Library of Congress)

Coffee joined him on the march, bringing with him a few hundreds of bushels of corn, and reporting that he had destroyed some Indian towns, but had encountered none of the Indians. The corn was a mere handful among the men and horses of the army, but cries for help were coming every hour from the friendly Indians, whose situation at the Ten Islands was desperate, and Jackson marched forward, trusting to chance for supplies. He meant to fight first and find something to eat afterward.

On the 28th of October, General Andrew Jackson sent Colonel Henry Dyer with a detachment of 200 men to capture the town of Littafuchee, located on the headwaters of Canoe Creek, between present day Ashville and Springville in St. Clair County. They surprised the Creek inhabitants before daylight in the morning and the village was burned. Twenty-eight Creeks, consisting of men, women and children were sent to Huntsville. The town was located on the headwaters of Canoe Creek, between Ashville and Springville in St. Clair County.

Major Battles

Battle Of Tallaseehatchee

On the 2nd day of November, Jackson learned that a considerable force of the enemy was gathered at Tallaseehatchee, a Native American town about ten miles from Ten Islands. He sent General Coffee, accompanied by Richard Brown and his company of Creeks and Cherokees, to attack the Red Stick stronghold. The town was situated near the head of the creek of that name, about three miles southwest of Jacksonville. It had about one hundred families, and a fighting force of one hundred and twenty warriors, that had recently been increased by three hundred warriors which brought together a force of four hundred and twenty fighting men.

General Coffee surrounded the town about sunrise of November 3rd. The engagement was swift and bloody. Not a Red Stick asked to be spared. There is some discrepancy in the accounts of those engaged, but the Native Americans killed were one hundred eighty-six warriors who were counted, and eighteen women. A number were never counted. Some escaped, and fled toward Oakfushee.

General Coffee's official report stated the following:

They made all the resistance that an overpowered soldier could do—they fought as long as one existed, but their destruction was very soon completed. Our men rushed up to the doors of the houses and in a few minutes killed the last warrior of them. The enemy fought with savage fury and met death with all its horrors, without shrinking or complaining—not one asked to be spared, but fought as long as they could stand or sit.

General Coffee's losses were five killed and 41 wounded. Eighty-four women and children, and fourteen hopelessly crippled warriors were taken prisoners. The prisoners were sent to Huntsville. On the same day, General Coffee returned to headquarters.

Of their arms and equipment in this battle. Brewer says—"A noticeable circumstance in connection with this battle is that the Indians were all armed with a bow and quiver of arrows, besides guns, which showed that they had taken to heart the advice of Tecumseh to throw aside the arts they had learned from the whites, and return to their primitive customs."

General Coffee (Library of Congress)

Buell says, p. 304: "An interesting feature of this encounter was the fact that it was Coffee's first battle. In his conduct of it, however, he exhibited skill and precision worthy a veteran of many fields. Coffee was an instinctive soldier, an intuitive general. Long after when his native capacity had been developed in many hard-fought encounters, including the battle of the 23rd below New Orleans, Gen. Jackson said of him: 'John Coffee is a consummate commander. He was born so. But he is so modest that he doesn't know it.'"

On the death of Gen. Coffee in 1834, Gov. William Carroll of Tennessee said of him in a funeral eulogy: "In view of all the circumstances, I had rather have been the hero of Tallaseehatchee than of the Horseshoe Bend. I had almost said New Orleans itself! It was the first battle of the Creek campaign; the first battle fought by any troops under Andrew Jackson's command. Upon its issue depended in great measure the morale of our troops, their confidence in their leaders and the buoyancy of spirit that would nerve them to endure the indescribable fatigues and privations to which they were subjected."— Buell, p. 305.

Mr. Parton, in his *Life of Andrew Jackson*, preserves a story which grew out of this battle:

On the bloody field of Tallashatchee was found a slain mother still embracing her living infant. The child was brought into camp with the other prisoners, and Jackson, anxious to save it, endeavored to induce some of the Indian women to give it nourishment. 'No,' said they, 'all his relatives are dead; kill him too.

This reply appealed to the heart of the general. He caused the child to be taken to his own hut, where among the few remaining stores was found a little brown sugar. This, mingled with water, served to keep the child alive until it could be sent to Huntsville, where it was nursed at Jackson's expense until the end of the campaign, and then taken to the Hermitage. Mrs. Jackson received it cordially, and the boy grew up in the family, treated by the general and his kind wife as a son and a favorite.

Lincoyer was the name given him by the general. He grew to be a finely formed and robust youth, and received the education usually given to the planters' sons in the neighborhood. Yet it appears he remained an Indian to the last, delighting to roam the fields and woods, and decorate his hair and clothes with gay feathers, and given to strong yearnings for his native wilds. The boy did not live to reach manhood, however. In his seventeenth year he fell a victim to pulmonary consumption, and when he died his benefactor mourned him as bitterly as if he had been indeed his son.

Jackson Protects Friendly Creeks

General Jackson continued to wait for supplies while camped at Fort Strother. General Cocke had been ordered to East Tennessee to procure supplies for the whole force and they never came. Men went into forests and shot game when possible but there was never enough food and a threat of a mutiny among his men.

In November, a friendly Native American arrived with word that the friendly Creek town of Talladega was in danger of being overwhelmed by over one thousand Red Stick warriors. The Native Americans at Talladega had refused to join the hostiles and in consequence they were attacked and had been driven into the stockade.

When General Jackson heard of the attack, even with an army badly in need of rations, he at once marched to its relief. On the morning of November 9th, his intrepid Tennesseans moved upon the enemy forces from the common center. The body of hostile Creeks were attempting to reduce what was known as Leslie's Station. This was a trading post at the old Indian town of Talladega, situated on a hill about a quarter of a mile southwest of the big spring and near the present town of Talladega.

The trading post was named after Alexander L. Leslie, the half Native American son of Alexander F. Leslie, a Scotch-Indian countryman in the Creek nation. The station was occupied by seventeen white men and about one hundred and twenty friendly Creeks, under the leadership of Jim Fife and Chinnabee.

The Red Sticks fought bravely, and at first repulsed the militia brigade, but they in turn were beaten back by fresh troops. The Tennesseans, under Jackson and his courageous lieutenants, pressed steadily forward. The Red Sticks gave way and numbers escaped though Jackson's lines. Many were pursued and shot down as they ran. The battle lasted scarcely more than an hour and a half.

For miles around, the woods were filled with dead and wounded warriors. Two hundred and ninety-nine Red Sticks were wounded on the battlefield proper, and there were doubtless many others that were not located. Jackson's losses were fifteen killed and eighty wounded. The forces of General Jackson consisted of about two thousand men, infantry and mounted, while the Red Sticks had about one thousand. The garrison in the fort was thus relieved. Jackson's dead were buried on the field.[7]

The hostile Creeks in that quarter had been routed with heavy loss, and the little band of beleaguered friendly Indians were released from their dangerous and trying situation; but Jackson's army was hungry, and there was a prospect that actual starvation would presently overtake it. The little food that was found at Talladega was distributed among the men, sufficing to satisfy their immediate needs.

It was important that the troops should return with all possible haste to Fort Strother, which should not be left in its defenseless state a moment longer than was absolutely necessary; but an instantaneous beginning of the return march was out of the question. The men had begun their toilsome journey at midnight between the 7th and 8th of November, and had marched all day on the 8th and, after a few hours' rest, had begun to march again a little after midnight, to go into battle early on the morning of the 9th. Now that the battle was done, they were utterly worn out, and needed rest. Accordingly, the army went into camp for the night, after they had buried their dead comrades. The next day the return march was begun, and on the 10th of November the weary army finally arrived at their encampment.

Luckily, the fort was unharmed, but it was still destitute of provisions, and for a time it was with great difficulty that Jackson prevented a mutiny among the troops, whose only food was the meagre supply gleaned from the surrounding wilderness.

---

7 The Talladega chapter, Daughters of the American Revolution, have had the remains removed to the city cemetery, where they were re-interred, and a handsome monument erected in commemoration of their valor.

Hillabee Massacre

An attack by the American forces under Gen. James White occurred on November 18th, 1813, in which large numbers of the Hillabee Indians were killed or captured, and their town devastated.

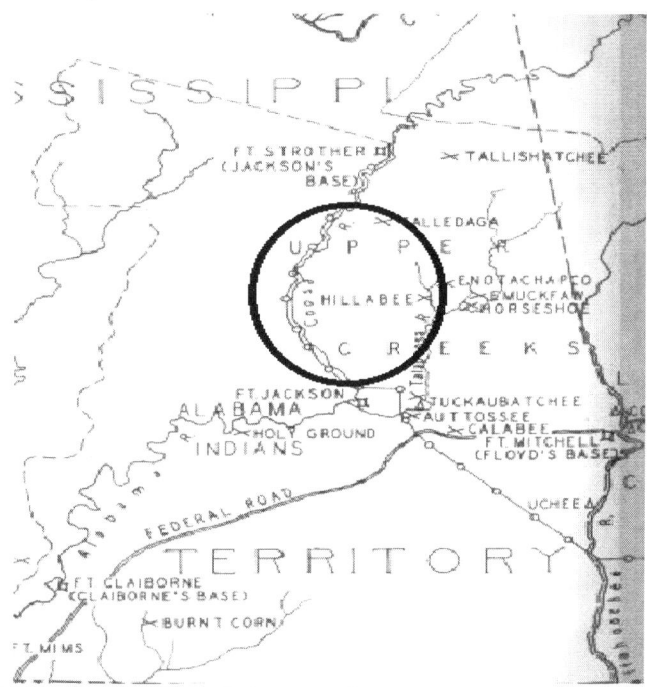

Map with location of the Hillabees in the Mississippi Territory (Library of Congress)

A portion of the Hillabees fought General John Coffee at Tallaseehatchee, and General Jackson at Talladega. These two defeats had such an effect that they sent a delegation to the latter at Fort Strother suing for peace, and expressing a willingness to agree to any terms that he might dictate. The delegation arrived there probably about November 16th, 1813. The spokesman appears to have been Robert Grayson, a Scotch-Indian countryman, long resident among the Hillabees.

Gen. Jackson received them, with the statement that the Government would only conclude its campaign among the Indians when they were completely subdued. Continuing he said:

"Upon those who are disposed to become friendly, I neither wish nor intend to make war; but they must afford evidences of the sincerity of their professions; the prisoners and property they have taken from us, and the friendly Creeks must be restored; the instigators of the war and the murderers of our citizens must be surrendered; the latter must and will be made to feel the force of our resentment. Long shall they remember Fort Mims in bitterness and tears."

General Jackson wrote to General Cocke, then at the mouth of Chattooga, informing him of the attitude of the Hillabees and of the nature of his reply, and remonstrating against General James White's proposed expedition against the Hillabees. He was too late, however, as that officer had already begun his march on November 11th.

General Jackson's "peace talk" never reached the Hillabees. Gen. White's force of a regiment of mounted infantry under Colonel Burch, a cavalry battalion under Major James P. H. Porter, and three hundred Cherokees under Colonel Gideon Morgan rapidly penetrated the Creek country, destroying the towns of Okfuskudshi (Little Okfuski) and Atchina-algi (Genalga) and sparing Enitachopco, in the belief that it might be of some use to the Americans in the future.

They found themselves in the vicinity of Hillabee town on November 17th located on the west side of Little Hillabee Creek, about a quarter of a mile away, and about six hundred yards a little west of north of Broken Arrow Creek. Its precise location was in the south central part of the northeast quarter of Sec. 12, T. 24, R. 21 E., in Tallapoosa County. It is said that this town might be at the time considered a sort of hospital, for in its cabins were about sixty-five helpless warriors who had been severely wounded at Tallasseehatchee and Talladega. Apart from these men, the only other occupants were women and children.

On the morning of November 18th, the very day on which General Jackson had given the Hillabee delegates his "peace talk" at Fort Strother, General White surrounded the town. The troops dismounted, entered the cabins and in ten or fifteen minutes bayonetted every one of the sixty-five helpless warriors. There was no resistance, and not an American was hurt. Just then someone in the town raised a white flag and General White's easy victory was supplemented by the surrender of twenty-five women and children. After burning the town the troops with their prisoners took up the line of march to Fort Armstrong.

General John Hartwell Cocke (Wikipedia)

Fort Mims was a battle and a massacre; the Hillabee affair was a massacre only.

General Jackson was both enraged and grieved when he heard of what had been done, and no doubt General White would have met with summary treatment if he had returned with his command to Fort

Strother. He doubtless knew this, and went to his home in east Tennessee.

This massacre for many months seriously affected the reputation of General Jackson in the eyes of the all the Native Americans, as it was supposed to have been done under his orders. Without a knowledge of the facts, they believed him guilty of treachery in permitting what they termed a murder of their wounded and helpless warriors. At the treaty of Fort Jackson, nine months later, one of the first acts of General Jackson, before entering upon negotiations, was to make a satisfactory explanation to the Creek delegates.

The Hillabee massacre had a most disastrous influence among the Creeks otherwise. It discouraged the friendly Native Americans, exasperated the lukewarm, and infused a spirit of despair into the hearts of the hostiles. With the latter there was never afterwards the slightest friendly overtures.

One historian describing the workings of the heart of the Native Americans says:

"From that time to the end of the war, it was observed that the Indians fought with greater fury and persistence than before; for they fought with the blended energy of hatred and despair. There was no suing for peace, no asking for quarter. They fought as long as they could stand, and as much longer as they could sit or kneel, and then as long as they had strength to shoot an arrow or pull a trigger—were all that they supposed remained to them after the destruction of the Hillabees."

Autosee Battle By Georgians

Red Eagle sent two bodies of his warriors to harass the borders of the future state of Alabama, one force threatened Tennessee and the other sought to find some vulnerable point on the Georgia frontier. When the call was made by General Claiborne upon Tennessee for assistance, a similarly earnest appeal was sent to Georgia, and the response from that state was equally prompt.

Jackson's advance with an overwhelming force and his vigorous blows at Tallaseehatchee and Talladega compelled the Creeks to abandon their designs upon Tennessee and stand upon the defensive. The other column, which threatened Georgia, was met in like manner by General Floyd, and with like results.

General Floyd of Georgia (Library of Congress)

Floyd's army from Georgia consisted of nine hundred and fifty militiamen and four hundred friendly Indians, part of them being Cowetas under command of Major McIntosh, one of the half-Native

Chief McIntosh (Alabama Department of Archives and History)

Americans whom High Head Jim had planned to kill and the rest were commanded by Tookabatchas under Mad Dragon's son.

Floyd was better equipped with some small pieces of artillery than Jackson had been in his first battles. Having learned that a large force of the Creeks was at High Head Jim's town, Autosse, on the south-east side of the Tallapoosa River, about twenty miles above the point at which that stream unites with the Coosa, General Floyd marched against them in the latter part of November.

Eggleston states that Floyd crossed the Ockmulgee, Flint, and Coosa rivers under the guidance of a Jewish trader named Abram Mordecai, and arrived in the neighborhood of Autosse early in the morning on the 29th of November.

His plan of battle was the same as that which Coffee had adopted at Tallaseehatchee (Tallushatchee), and Jackson at Talladega. He planned to surround the town and destroy the fighting force within, but their scheme failed.

"In the first place, McIntosh and Mad Dragon's son were ordered to cross the river and cut off retreat to the opposite shore, and they failed to do what was required of them. Whether this was due to the unforeseen difficulties of crossing, as the Native Americans alleged; or to the reluctance of the Red Sticks to swim the river on a cold, frosty morning, as some historians say; or to a failure of their courage, as was charged at the time —there are now no means of determining, and it is not important. It is enough to know that they did not cross the river as ordered, and hence when the attack was made the bank of the stream opposite the town was unguarded."

The real position and strength of the Red Stick force had been miscalculated, and when this was discovered, General Floyd was obliged to alter his plans.

"The advance was made as soon as there was sufficient light, on the morning of the 29th of November, with Booth's battalion on the right, Watson's on the left. The flanks were guarded by riflemen, and Thomas with his artillery accompanied Booth's battalion. Booth was instructed to march until he could rest the head of his column upon the little creek at the mouth of which the town stood, while Watson was to stretch his column around to the left in a curve, resting its left flank upon the river just below the town. If this could have been done as intended, and the friendly Indians had occupied the opposite side of the river, the encircling of the place would have been complete; but besides the failure of the Indians another difficulty stood in the way."

Floyd realized that instead of one town there were two, and the second was lying about a quarter of a mile further down the river, immediately in rear of the position to which Watson had been ordered.

"General Floyd sent Lieutenant Hendon with Merriweather's riflemen, three, companies of infantry and two of dragoons to attack the lower town, while he threw the remainder of the army, now reinforced by the friendly Indians under Mad Dragon's son and Mcintosh, against the larger upper town."

The fighting began about sunrise, and quickly became severe. The prophets made the place sacred ground, and they had assured the warriors that any white force which should attack them would be utterly exterminated, so the Red Sticks resisted the attack with terrible determination, contesting every inch of the ground which they believed to be sacred.

Soon after the battle began, the artillery—an arm which was particularly dreaded by the Creeks with something of superstitious horror—was brought forward and unlimbered. Its rapid discharges soon turned the tide of battle. Then Major Freeman with his squadron of cavalry charged and broke their lines.

Floyd's infantry pressed the Red Sticks, while the friendly Indians who had now crossed the creek cut off retreat up the river, leaving the broken and flying Creeks no road of escape except across the river.

"At nine o'clock both towns were in flames, and there was no army in Floyd's front. He was victor in the action, and his success in attacking a sacred stronghold was certain to work great demoralization among the superstitious Creeks; but prudence dictated a retreat nevertheless."

The country round about was populated with Native Americans, and the force which fought at Autosse although broken was not destroyed. It was certain that if the army remained in the neighborhood it was in danger of being beaten by the superior force which the Creeks could speedily muster.

Additionally, Floyd had only a scanty supply of provisions, and his base of supplies was sixty miles away, on the Chattahoochie River. He marched his men as soon as he could bury his dead and arrange for the care of his wounded, of whom he was himself one.

On the return march, Red Sticks attacked Floyd's rear within a mile of their burned town on the day of the battle. However, their numbers were not sufficient to enable them to fight for an extended period.

In the battle of Autosse Floyd lost eleven white men killed and fifty-four wounded, besides some losses among his friendly Indians. The exact number of the slain warriors of the enemy was not ascertained, but it was estimated at about two hundred.

Holy Ground Campaign And Battle

The principal campaign and engagement between the Creeks and the whites in South Alabama, continued for several weeks, and concluded with the battle of the Holy Ground, December 23, 1813.

The Holy Ground, (also spelled Econachaca & Ikanatchaka) was an Indian town of controlling influence among the Indians, during the Creek Indian War of 1813-14. It was located between Pintlala and Big Swamp Creek, on the Alabama River in the present Lowndes County and was about two miles north of White Hall.

Map shows location of Holy Ground in the center (Library of Congress)

The town contained the council house of the Alabama tribe, and was the residence of the principal Creek prophets, who with their magic spells at the opening of the War, had asserted that it had been made holy or was consecrated against the intrusion of white men. Until its destruction, it was a base for provisions and war supplies of the Creeks in their operations against the settlers.

General F. L. Claiborne, then in south Alabama, resolved that the Holy Ground must be destroyed. Accordingly, he prepared to march there against the protest from his officers. They complained of their poor condition for such an undertaking. Their force was weak in numbers, ill sorted, and in fact rather unwilling to go.

Nine captains, eight lieutenants, and five ensigns sent him a written remonstrance against what they believed to be the mad undertaking. These officers directed their commander's attention to several ugly facts with respect to his situation. They reminded him that the weather was cold and inclement; that the troops were badly shod and insufficiently supplied with clothing; that there was scarcely a possibility of feeding them regularly upon so long a march into the literally pathless forest; and finally that the term of service for which many of the men had enlisted would soon come to an end. The remonstrance was earnest but perfectly respectful. The officers who signed it assured General Claiborne that if he should adhere to his determination they would go with him without murmuring and do their duty. As there was nothing set forth in the remonstrance which Claiborne did not know or had not duly considered already, it made no change in his mind.

In November, 1813, he marched with his army from the Tombigbee to Weatherford's Bluff on the Alabama, where he established a depot of provisions for General Jackson, and erected a fort, to which the name Fort Claiborne was given and the town of Claiborne inherited it's name. Here on November 28th, his army was re-enforced by the 3rd United States Infantry Regiment under Colonel Gilbert Christian Russell.

On December 13th, in obedience to instructions from Gen. Thomas Flournoy, General Claiborne advanced his forces from Fort Claiborne toward the Holy Ground. After several days' march a brief halt was made in the present Butler County, where a depot was established, known as Fort Deposit. He left his wagons, cannon, baggage, and the sick there, with one hundred men as a guard. The march was then resumed.

In the Holy Ground there were as many as two hundred houses, and during the two or three months which had elapsed since the town was established many of the prisoners taken by the Red Sticks in battle had been brought there and murdered. When Claiborne advanced to attack the place, preparations were being made in the public square for the burning of a number of unfortunate captives, among whom were a white woman named Mrs. Sophia Durant and several friendly half-Native Americans.

The Red Sticks, on learning of the approach of Gen. Claiborne's army, took the precautions to move their women and children across the Alabama River into what is now Autauga County. They thus evidenced their unwillingness to put much faith in their vaunted belief as to the impregnability of the town.

About midday December 23rd, the town was attacked. As Claiborne's troops poured into the city along the left bank of the river, the center column under Colonel Carson curved outward like a crescent. Each man's face was set hard with purpose. Amid a frenzied outburst of shouts and yells and beating of drums, the Creek warriors rushed out to meet the Americans, while smaller groups fired on them behind heavy log breastworks. It was for the "entire nation as well as for the Holy City, for which the Indians now fought, and not until the galling fire from Claiborne's men had begun to decimate their ranks did they begin a retreat."[8]

The battle lasted only about one hour, resulting in a complete defeat, the Red Sticks made good their escape across the river, and left thirty-three warriors slain. The number of wounded is not known, as they succeeded in bearing them all away.

William Weatherford, (Red Eagle) had conducted the defense of the Holy Ground, and was one of the last to make an escape. It was from here that

---

8   Rowland, Dunbar, Publications of the Mississippi Historical Society: Centenary series, Volume 4, 1921

Red Eagle made his famous horseback leap from the river bluff while making his escape that became one of the most picturesque incidents of the Creek War.

Historican Albert J. Pickett describes Weatherford's leap in his *History of Alabama* with the following account which he assured was from Red Eagle's own lips:

"Coursing with great rapidity along the banks of the Alabama, below the town, on a gray steed of unsurpassed strength and fleetness, which he had purchased a short time before the commencement of hostilities of Benjamin Baldwin, late of Macon County, [he] came at length to the termination of a kind of ravine, where there was a perpendicular bluff ten or fifteen feet above the surface of the river. Over this with a mighty bound the horse pitched with the gallant chief, and both went out of sight beneath the waves. Presently they rose again, the rider having hold of the mane with one hand and his rifle firmly grasped in the other. Regaining his saddle, the noble animal swam with him to the Autauga side."

Another description of the incident, worthy of a romance novel, was given by Major Dreisbach:

When Weatherford found that most of his warriors had deserted him, he thought of his own safety. Finding himself hedged in above and below on the river, he determined to cross the Alabama. He was mounted on a horse of almost matchless strength and fleetness and with the swiftness of the wind turned down a long hollow that led to the bank of the river; on his arrival he found the bluff about twelve feet high; he took in at a glance the situation and determined to make the leap. He rode back about thirty paces and turned his horse's head towards the bluff, and then, with touch of the spur and the sharp 'ho ya' of his voice, he put the noble animal to the top of his speed and dashed over the bluff full twenty feet into the flashing waters below, which opened its bosom to receive the dauntless hero, who sought its sparkling waves as a barrier between him and the pursuing foe. He did not lose his seat; his horse and the lower part of his own body went entirely under the water, he holding his rifle high above his head. The gallant horse struck out for the opposite shore with his fearless rider upon his back. When he had advanced some thirty yards from the shore, the *balls from the guns of the troopers who were above and below him began to spatter around him like hail, but it appeared that the "Great Spirit" watched over him, for not a shot struck either man or horse. As soon as he reached the farther shore he dismounted and took off his saddle and examined his brave and noble horse to see if he had been struck. One shot had cut off a bunch or lock of the horse's mane just in front of the saddle. Finding his noble "Arrow" unhurt, he resaddled him and mounted, and sending back a note of defiance, rode off, to fight again on other ensanguined fields.*

The American loss at the Holy Ground was one killed and twenty wounded. This extremely light loss, considering the bravery with which the Creeks fought, must be ascribed to the scarcity of ammunition among them, which compelled many of the warriors to have resort to bows and arrows.

The spoils of the Holy Ground were given by General Claiborne to his Choctaw allies under Pushmatahaw, and the town was then burned. The two succeeding days were devoted to the destruction of other towns of the Holy Ground and vicinity and the enemy farms and boats.

The army was now reduced almost to starvation, their only food being a little corn, which they parched and ate as they could. An alarm was given by a party of men who were sent up the river in pursuit of fugitives. Claiborne marched in that direction during the night of December 24th, and pitched his tent on Weatherford's plantation where he ate his Christmas breakfast of parched corn. While at Weatherford's plantation, a letter was found from Governor Manique of Pensacola which congratulated Red Eagle on his victory at Fort Mims.

Having destroyed all the buildings in the neighborhood, Claiborne's work in this region was done, and he hastened back to Fort Deposit, where he fed his troops before beginning his return march to Fort Claiborne. The army had been nine days without meat.

"The news of the fall of the capital of the Creek Nation instantly spread all over the country, from house to house and town to town, and everywhere on the frontiers in camp and in assembly halls, Claiborne's victory was applauded and celebrated, bonfires flaming along the whole eastern frontier and far into the interior of the Mississippi Territory. Not even the great Jackson had won so distinctive a victory, nor had he, as yet, met Weatherford anywhere on the battlefield. The signal victory of Holy Ground, however, was not to be without its sacrifice. The men were returning to Camp Vernon in a pitiable condition, half naked, bare-footed and hungry, to face a failure of crops on arriving home. On Christmas Day they with their beloved General had dined on parched corn and boiled acorns. He was returning with them broken in health from exposure, and suffering from wounds from which he never recovered. On January 14, 1814, he wrote the following from Camp Mount Vernon."[9]

My volunteers are returning to their homes with eight months' pay due them and almost literally naked. They have served the last three months of inclement winter weather without shoes or blankets, almost without shirts, but are still devoted to their country and properly impressed with the justice and the necessity of the war.

The defeat of the Creeks at the Holy Ground closed their military operations in South Alabama, and it tended greatly to facilitate the work of General Jackson in bringing the war to a close three months later by the decisive Battle of the Horseshoe Bend. After this battle the army returned to Fort Claiborne where many of the volunteers were honorably discharged, their term of service having expired.

---

9 Rowland, Dunbar, Publications of the Mississippi Historical Society: Centenary series, Volume 4, 1921

Threat Of Starvation Men Turn To Mutiny

Leaving Colonel Russell in command of Fort Claiborne, General Claiborne returned to Mount Vernon, partly because he had fully accomplished all that his orders from Flournoy permitted him to do, and partly because the discharge of his Mississippi volunteers had reduced his army to sixty men, and even these had but a month longer to serve.

Colonel Russell was no sooner left in command at Fort Claiborne than he instituted proceedings designed to fix the responsibility for the sufferings of the men during the campaign. He ordered a court of inquiry in each case. Major Cassels was permitted to escape censure on the ground that his guide had misled him. For the failure of the food supply the contractor was held responsible, as it was shown that General Claiborne had given him strict orders to provide abundant supplies for the expedition.

In February following the events at Fort Claiborne, it was Colonel Russell's purpose to march to the Old Towns on the Cahawba River, and to attack the Red Sticks wherever he could find them, and to establish his base of supplies at that point. He provided a barge, loaded it with food for the troops, and putting Captain Denkins in command of it, with a piece of artillery as his armament, he directed that officer to ascend the Alabama River to the mouth of the Cahawba River, and then to make his way up the Cahawba to Old Towns, where the army would meet him. There, with his regiment reinforced by an infantry company from the neighborhood of Fort Madison under command of Captain Evan Austill, and a cavalry company commanded by Captain Foster—the two forming a battalion under the lead of Sam Dale, who was now a Major—Colonel Russell marched to the appointed place of rendezvous.

When he arrived, he learned that the barge had not arrived, and as he had marched with only six days of provisions his situation was a critical one. To hasten the coming of the barge he sent a canoe manned by Lieutenant Wilcox and five men in search of Captain Denkins. This party, while making its way down the river, traveling at night and hiding in the cane on the banks by day, was attacked by Indians. Lieutenant Wilcox and three of his companions were made prisoners, the other two escaped and made their way through many hardships to the settlements, where they arrived in a famished condition.

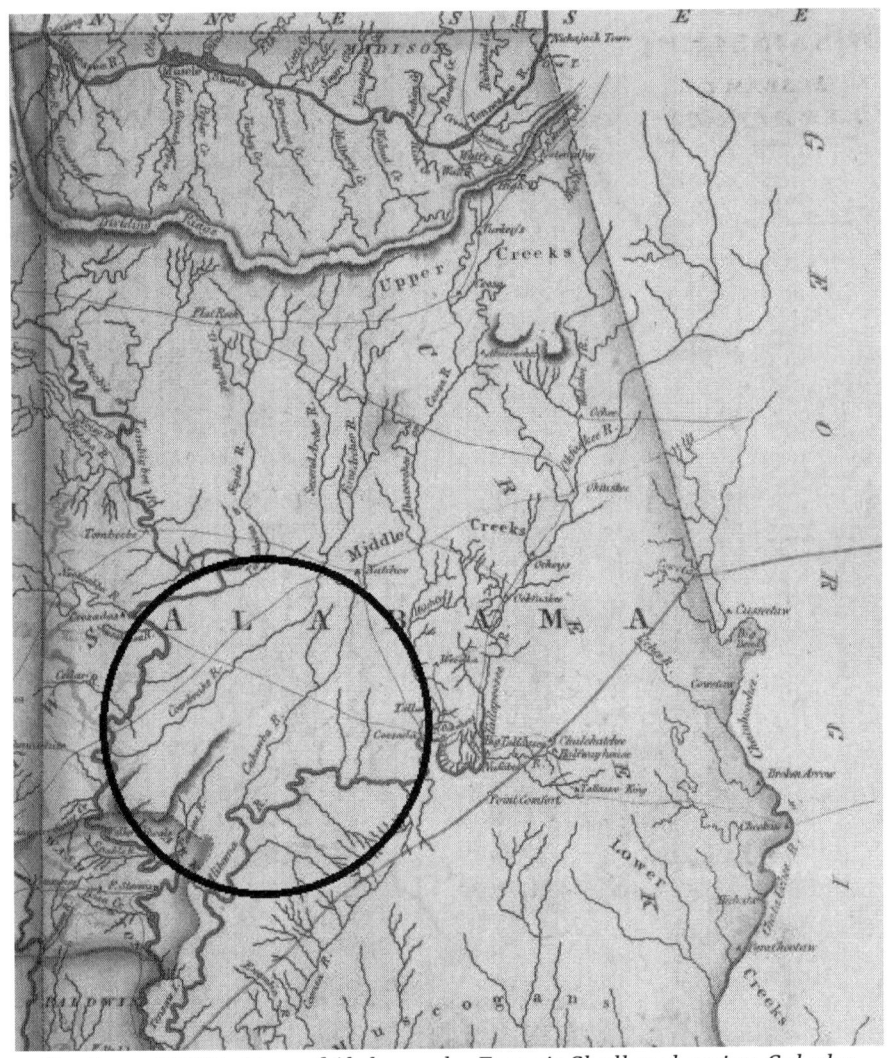

Portion of 1800s Map of Alabama by Francis Shallus showing Cahaba River (Library of Congress)

Captain Denkins passed the mouth of the Cahawba River by mistake, and gone a considerable distance up the Alabama River before discovering his error. When he discovered it, he knew that it was now too late for him to think of carrying out his original instructions. He knew that before he could possibly reach the Old Towns, the army would be starved out and compelled to retreat so he decided to return to Fort Claiborne. On his way down the river he discovered a canoe, and found in it Wilcox scalped and dying, and his two companions already dead.

Meantime Colonel Russell had waited two days at the Old Towns for the coming of the barge. Finally, being wholly without provisions, his was forced to start his return march and only managed to save his army from starvation by killing and eating his horses on the route.

The situation at Fort Storther near Ten Islands was not any better at General Jackson's camp. From the time of the Talladega Battle to Holy Ground, food provisions had grown steadily worse. Jackson lost no opportunity to secure such provisions as could be had from the surrounding country, but these were barely sufficient to keep famine at bay from day to day, and Jackson busied himself with the writing of letters to everybody who could in any way contribute to hasten forward adequate supplies. He wrote to one contractor, saying:

I have been compelled to return here for the want of supplies when I could have completed the destruction of the enemy in ten days; and on my arrival I find those I had left behind in the same starving condition with those who accompanied me. For God's sake send me with all dispatch plentiful supplies of bread and meat. We have been starving for several days, and it will not do to continue so much longer. Hire wagons and purchase supplies at any price rather than defeat the expedition. General White, instead of forming a junction with me, as he assured me he would, has taken the retrograde motion, after having amused himself with consuming provisions for three weeks in the Cherokee Nation, and left me to rely on my own strength.

Day by day food became scarcer, poorer, and more difficult to get, and the men were becoming mutinous, as volunteers are sure to do when left to starve in inaction. As it was, there was neither food nor fighting to be had at Fort Strother, and General Jackson did not dare to attempt a march upon the nearest Indian stronghold, about sixty miles away, without supplies.

Jackson knew that the men would not leave singly, that their pride would restrain them from desertion unless they could act together, each being sustained by the opinion and the common action of all his fellows. The militia had determined to march home in a body and Jackson determined to restrain them in a body.

On the appointed day they planned to desert, he called the volunteers to arms and at their head placed himself in the way of the mutinous militiamen. He plainly informed the men that they could march homeward only by cutting their way through his lines, and this was an undertaking which they were not prepared for. Being unable to overcome Jackson, they had no choice but to yield to him and return to their tents with what cheerfulness they could command.

Print of Jackson quelling the mutiny ca. 1843 (Library of Congress)

The volunteers whose power Jackson was able to use in stopping the departure of the militia were scarcely less discontented than they. On the very day on which they stopped the march of the militia they resolved themselves to go home, and prepared to depart on the following morning. Jackson had information of what was going on, and he prepared to reverse the order of things by using the militia in their turn to oppose the volunteers. The militia having returned to their duty obeyed the commands of their general, and revealed a firm front to the mutinous volunteers. The affair wore so much of the appearance of a practical joke that it put the whole force into momentary good-humor.

However, the supplies did not arrive and the men remained discontented. Finally, Jackson asked for two days' delay, promising to permit the men to march away if food did not arrive within that time. Two days passed and still no food arrived. Jackson knew he had to let them go, but grasping at straws, he declared that if even two men would consent to stay with him, then he would not abandon Fort Strother and the campaign. Immediately, one of his captains agreed to stay as one of this army of two, and finally the number of volunteers who agreed to stay swelled to one hundred and nine men. This was all that was left of Jackson's army, and a good deal of the campaign lay ahead.

Jackson permitted the rest of the troops to leave, but demanded that they return if they met with the supply train. In order to enforce his demand, he accompanied the column and left the one hundred and nine volunteers to hold down the fort until his return.

The column met the provision train twelve miles from the fort, so Jackson called a halt and issued rations to the men. With their stomachs filled with beef and bread, Jackson ordered the men to return to the fort, but the troops refused and started homeward instead.

Historian George Cary Eggleston in his *Red Eagle: And the Wars with the Creek Indians of Alabama*, describes one of the most impressive scenes in Jackson's career. Eggleston states the following:

Raving with rage, his thin lips set and his frame quivering with anger, the commander's face and mien were terrible. His left arm was still carried in a sling, and the hardships, hunger, fatigue, and ceaselesss anxiety to which he had been subject ever since he quitted his sick-bed to come upon this campaign had not made his wasted frame less emaciated; he was a sick man who ought to have been in bed: but the illness was of the body, not of the soul. The spirit of the man was now intensely stirred, and when Jackson was in this mood there were few men who had the courage to brave him.

Riding after the head of the column, he placed himself with a few followers in front of it, and drove the men back like sheep. Then leaving the officers who were with him he rode alone down the road, until he encountered a brigade which was drawn up in column, resolved to conquer its way by a regular advance against any body of men who might oppose its homeward march. If a company or a battalion had undertaken to arrest the march of these men there would have been a battle there in the road without question. They were prepared to fight their comrades to the death; they were ready to meet a force equal to their own. They met Andrew Jackson instead—Andrew Jackson in a rage, Andrew Jackson with all the blood in his frail body boiling; and that was a force greatly superior to their own.

Snatching a musket from one of the men Jackson commanded the mutineers to halt. He broke forth in a torrent of vituperation, and declared that they could march toward home only over his dead body; he declared, too, with an emphasis which carried conviction with it, that while he could not, single-handed, overcome a brigade of armed men, he at least could and would shoot down the first man who should dare to make the least motion toward advancing.

The men were overawed, terrified, demoralized by the force of this one resolute man's fierce determination. They stood like petrified men, not knowing what to do. It was now evident that no man there would dare to make himself Jackson's target by being the first to advance. Jackson had beaten a brigade, literally single-handed, for he had but one hand that he could use.

By this time General Coffee and some staff officers had joined Jackson, and now a few of the better disposed men, seeing their general opposing a brigade of mutineers, ranged themselves by his side, prepared to assist him in any encounter that might come, however badly over-matched they might be. The mutineers were already conquered, however, and sullenly yielding they were sent back to the fort."

Jackson continued on to Fort Deposit and succeeded in arranging for a constant supply of bread and meat. Then he returned to Fort Strother. However, his success was short-lived because he discovered on his return that the volunteers were planning a new mutiny because they had completed the year for which they had enlisted which would end on December 10th. On the evening of the 9th, word came that the men were already strapping their knapsacks on their backs and getting ready to march immediately.

Jackson had to act. The scene that took place next is described by George Cary Eggleston.

Jackson issued one of the shortest of all his proclamations, ordering all good soldiers to assist in putting down the mutiny. Then he ordered the militia to parade at once under arms. Placing his cannon in a commanding position, he drew up the militia in-line of battle and confronted the mutinous volunteers.

Riding to the front he made a speech to the volunteers, beginning by assuring them that they could march only over his dead body; that he had done with entreaty, and meant now to use force; that they must now make their choice between returning to their tents and remaining quietly upon duty, and fighting him and his troops right where he stood; the point, he said, could be decided very quickly by arms if they chose to submit the question to that kind of argument. He told them, too, that he was expecting new troops to take their places, and that until these new troops should arrive not a man present should quit the post except by force.

He was now terribly in earnest, and bent upon no half-way measures. He had drawn his men up in line of battle, not as a threat, but for purposes of battle. He was ready to fight, and meant to fight, not defensively, but offensively. He wanted no negotiation, asked no man upon what terms he would submit. He had dictated the terms himself and meant now to enforce them. He had given the volunteers a choice—either to remain peaceably until he should send them home, or to fight a battle with him right there in the road and right then on the 9th of December; he had offered them this choice, and they must choose and say what their choice was. When he ended his speech the volunteers stood grimly, sullenly silent. They did not offer to advance, but that was not enough. They must say whether they would remain and obey, or accept battle. If they would promise to remain without further attempts of this kind, he was content; if not, the battle would begin.

"I demand an explicit answer," he said; and no reply coming, he turned to his artillerymen and ordered them to stand to their guns with lighted matches.

It was now a question merely of seconds. Jackson gave the men time to answer, but not many moments would pass before he would speak the only words which were left to him to speak—the words "commence firing," those words which in every battle are the signal for the transformation of iron or brazen guns from harmless cylinders of metal into bellowing monsters, belching fiery death from their throats.

There was silence for a moment—that awful silence which always precedes the turmoil of battle, doing more to appall men than all the demoniac noises of the contest do; then a murmur was heard as of men hastily consulting; then the officers of the volunteer brigade stepped a pace to the front and delivered the answer which Jackson had demanded.

They had made their choice, and the answer was that they would return to duty, and remain at the fort until the new men should come, or until their commander should receive authority to discharge them.

This affair of the 9th of December, 1813, is nowhere set down in the list of Jackson's battles; but nowhere did he win a more decided victory or display his qualities as a great commander to better advantage.

Jackson continued to have trouble keeping his soldiers while he waited on new troops to take their place. The militia finally left in spite of all that Jackson tried to do to detain them, and Cocke's volunteers followed them ten days afterward, but in the meantime a force of nine hundred new men had arrived. They had enlisted in part for two and in part for three months, and were therefore of comparatively little value; but Jackson resolved to use them at least while waiting for the arrival of the larger and better force which had been ordered to gather at Fayetteville on the 28th of January.

He meant to strike a blow with what force he had while its enlistment should continue, so that no more men might be paid for service as soldiers without doing any fighting. The volunteers whose term had expired marched out of camp on the 14th of January, and on the next day Jackson set his new men in motion for work. They were undrilled, undisciplined, and weak in numbers, but Jackson was now bent upon fighting with any thing that he could get which remotely resembled an army.

General Coffee Is Wounded

With the arrival of eight hundred and fifty newly arrived Tennessee volunteers at Fort Strother who had agreed to serve for sixty days, General Jackson's army was sufficiently increased in numbers for him to consider a battle.

About the same time General Jackson was informed by his scouts that a large force of Creeks had congregated in a bend of the Tallapoosa River near the mouth of Emuckfau Creek, and that they were planning an attack on Fort Armstrong on the Coosahatchie which was in present Cherokee County, and very near the Georgia line. This fort was garrisoned by some two hundred friendly Creeks and Cherokees, and eighteen or twenty white men from Mississippi.

General Jackson resolved to strike an immediate blow, not only to keep his men employed, but also to demoralize the Red Sticks. Coupled with his own determination and advice from General Pinckney and General Floyd, his troops set out to attack the Indians gathering on the Tallapoosa.

On January 15th about eight hundred mounted troops, crossed the Coosa River at Fish Dam Ford and marched to a good grazing ground on Wehogee Creek, four miles distant from Fort Strother, and there they camped.

The main force joined them the following day. which consisted of an artillery company, with one six-pounder, commanded by Lieutenant Robert Armstrong, a company of infantry, two companies of spies, commanded by Captain John Gordon and Captain William Russell, and a company of volunteer officers commanded by General Coffee. A small force only had been left at Fort Strother.

On January 17 they marched toward Talladega Fort, and reached it the next day. Here they were reinforced by two or three hundred friendly

Native Americans, including sixty-five Cherokees, the remainder Creeks. They received word that General Floyd was about to begin a movement, and also a letter from Colonel William Snodgrass, in which he stated that Fort Armstrong was about to be attacked. General Jackson immediately planned an advance. His men prepared three days' rations, and were otherwise put in marching order.

The movement against Emuckfau was begun on January 19th. The army camped on the next night at Enitachopco, at which a battle was later fought on January 24. On the night of the 21st, Jackson's troops had reached Emuckfau Creek. Disposing his men in a hollow square, pickets were placed, spies were sent out, and his camp fires built around but far beyond the camp. About 11 o'clock p. m. the spies reported that the Red Sticks were encamped three miles away, engaged in dancing, and with demonstrations, indicating that they knew General Jackson's presence. The men rested quietly on their arms throughout the night, awaiting the attack they knew was imminent.

At daybreak on January 22nd, the alarm guns of the sentinels, followed by the yells of the Red Sticks, announced the beginning of the expected battle. The Creeks made a furious assault on Jackson's left flank, by which it was met with great firmness. The battle continued for about a half an hour.

With the coming of dawn, the exact disposition of the Red Sticks was ascertained. General Jackson reinforced his left wing, and the whole line, under General Coffee, charged upon the Red Sticks. The friendly Native Americans joined in the chase and the Creeks were driven with great loss for about two miles.

The chase over, General Coffee was detached with four hundred men and the friendly Native Americans to burn the Creek encampment. They found it impracticable to do this without the aid of artillery since it was well-fortified so his party returned to camp.

About half an hour afterward, the battle was renewed by the Creeks attacking General Jackson's right flank in an attempt to draw the attention of the white troops and thus expose the left wing. This was met by General Coffee with two hundred men, but owing to some mistake in orders, only his old company of around fifty mounted volunteer officers followed him. With this small force he advanced upon the superior numbers of the enemy who were posted on a ridge. General Coffee dismounted his men, charged the lines, and drove them into a reed brake on the margin of the creek.

The main force of Native Americans which had been carefully concealed on the left, now made a sudden and violent assault upon the left wing, which they believed to have been weakened and demoralized by the first engagement. The charge was met with great firmness, and the Native Americans were repulsed.

The battle then became general along the whole line. The Red Sticks fought in the old way, every man adopting his own tactics, shooting from behind trees, logs, or from whatever shelter afforded the best protection, falling flat on the ground to reload, then rising to deliver the fire. General Coffee ordered his men to dismount and charge them, and they were driven back to the bank of a stream. The battle continued for some time. The friendly Native Americans had earlier in the engagement been ordered to the support of General Coffee, but when the attack became fiercest on the left wing, they joined with the fight in that quarter.

General Coffee had been fighting for an hour against a greatly superior force, so General Jackson dispatched Jim Fife, the principal Creek chief in charge of the friendly warriors, to his relief. General Coffee and the Creek chief charged in concert, and the enemy broke, losing forty-five men in the charge and pursuit of about three miles. General Coffee was shot and severely wounded in the attack. Major Donelson and three others were killed. The battle closed about the middle of the afternoon.

The battle over, the dead were collected and buried, the wounded given attention, and a temporary fortification thrown up about the camp. The main objects of the expedition had been accomplished. The Indians had been diverted from any possible attempt to re-enforce those against whom General Floyd advanced on the Tallapoosa, and Fort Armstrong was relieved from possible attack. In front of General Coffee's lines the bodies of forty-five warriors were found. A like proportion were killed in other parts of the battle.

Although a victor at Emuckfau, General Jackson did not feel that he could hold the ground taken with his limited force, and without supplies nearer than Talladega which was forty miles away. His soldiers had only one day's rations, and his Native American troops none. For two days and two nights his horses had been without food, other than occasional grazing. He therefore resolved to fall back to Talladega.

Litters were made from the skins of slain horses, on which the sick and wounded were carried. At 10 o'clock on the day following the battle, he began his return march, the troops in regular order, with sick and wounded in the center. That night they reached the village of Enitaochopco (also known as Anatichapko), where they camped.

Entire Rear Guard, Panic-Stricken, Had Plunged Into The Stream

On the night of January 23rd, 1814, General Jackson's army, fresh from the victory over the Indians at Emuckfau the previous day, but almost destitute of supplies, they were encamped near the Creek Indian village of Enitaohopco (also known as Anatichapko, and Enotacpapco)

The camp was on the south side of the creek of that name, and a quarter of a mile from the ford, at which they had previously crossed. The ford was a deep ravine between two hills covered with dense shrubbery. It afforded admirable opportunity for an ambush, and this General. Jackson so much feared, that another ford was found six hundred yards below the first.

On the morning of January 24th the march was resumed. The litters with the wounded were placed just behind the first guards. The three columns of the right, the left and the center were commanded respectfully by Colonels Perkins, Nicholas T. Stump, and William Carroll. Before the enemy was aware of this change in the Americans route, the advanced guard, the wounded, and a part of the center division had already crossed the stream. The single piece of artillery had entered the ford when the battle cry of the Muscogees was heard behind, and fired upon Captain Russell's company of spies which was bringing up the rear. The fire was returned.

General Jackson was in the stream when he heard the firing commence. He at once had an aide go forward and form a line for the protection of the wounded, and he turned back to the east bank. Here he discovered a most disgraceful condition.

Nearly the entire rear guard, panic-stricken, had plunged into the stream and were making their way to the other bank. Only a small force of about one hundred men remained on the east side, and their fighting was to prove an offset to the panic of the rest. The force left to bear the brunt were Captain Russell's company of spies, about twenty-five of the rear guard under Colonel Carroll and Captain Quarles, and Lieutenant Armstrong's artillery company. Captain Quarles soon fell. These gallant men and their comrades, with the greatest heroism, contended against many times their number.

Portion of Map with locations of Emuckfau and Enitaohopco (Library of Congress)

The Native Americans, realizing the American's situation, were jubilant because of the disorder.

At the first fire of the Red Sticks, Lieutenant Armstrong had ordered a part of his company to advance and take possession of a hill, then hold it with their muskets, while he and others dragged the six-pounder from the creek to the same point.

The rammer and pricker were left tied to the limber, but in spite of this mishap two of the gunners, Constantino Perkins and Craven Jackson, were equal to the emergency, Perkins using his musket in driving down the cartridges and Jackson using his ramrod in preparing them for the match. The cannon poured a fire of grapeshot into the ranks of the enemy. Again it was loaded and fired, and by it and with the fire of muskets, the Creeks were driven back.

General Jackson and his staff had, by very great exertion, somewhat restored order, and detachments were sent across to support the small force so bravely holding the crossing. Still, the enemy's balls fell thick and fast on the American ranks. Captain Hamilton had fallen, Captains Bradford and McGavock were down.

Captain Gordon's company of spies, which was leading the army and was well across the creek, now recrossed, striking the Red Sticks on the left as they were about to make on the cannon.

The artillery company suffered severely. Lieutenant Armstrong fell severely wounded, exclaiming "my brave boys, some of you may fall, but you must save the cannon."

The artillerists ascended the bank with the most determined obstinacy, loaded their gun under a shower of lead, and sent repeated charges of grape among the Muscogees.

Notwithstanding he was severely wounded at Emuckfau, General Coffee mounted his horse, and was of great service to General Jackson in stemming the tide of disaster, and encouraging the men to meet their duty. The tide of battle now began to turn. The Red Sticks could not withstand the increasing attacks. They broke at all points and fled, throwing away blankets, packs and everything else impeding their flight. They were pursued more than two miles.

The losses of the Americans in the battles of Emuckfau and Enitachopko, were twenty killed and seventy-five wounded. Some of the latter died. According to Buell the loss of the Creeks in these two battles was one hundred ninety-four killed, and more than two hundred wounded. The statement of General Jackson is that the bodies of one hundred and eighty-nine Native Americans were found dead. He reported that only a guess could be made as to the number of wounded. In Eaton the statement is made that it was afterwards learned from prisoners that more than two hundred warriors never returned from these engagements.

"In these several battles, the Muscogees fought with a courage worthy of a better fate, and their loss was accordingly severe." (General Floyd's Report)

The forces of the Creeks in each engagement were much less than the Americans. Pickett states that they had less than five hundred warriors. After burying the dead, General Jackson resumed his march without molestation, and on January 27th arrived at Fort Strother.

Notwithstanding their losses, and their consequent inability to pursue, the Red Sticks are stated, by Pickett, to have looked upon the retrograde movement of General Jackson into Fort Strother as indicating a victory for them They boasted that they "whipped Capt. Jackson and drove him to the Coosa River."

Georgia Volunteers Fight At Calabee

An engagement took place between the Georgia militia, under General Floyd and the Creek Indians, January 27, 1814, on Calebee Creek, about 7 miles from the present town of Tuskegee, Macon County, Alabama. After the battle of Autossee, November 29, 1813, and his retreat to Fort Mitchell, General. Floyd remained inactive about six weeks awaiting food and recovering from sickness.

On receiving necessary supplies, and recruiting his forces, with about 1,227 men, a company of cavalry, and 400 friendly Native Americans, he set out on another campaign. He moved slowly along the line of the old federal road, pausing to establish forts at intervals so that a line of defensive posts would lie like a trail behind him, protecting his line of communications and affording convenient places for the storage and safe keeping of supplies.

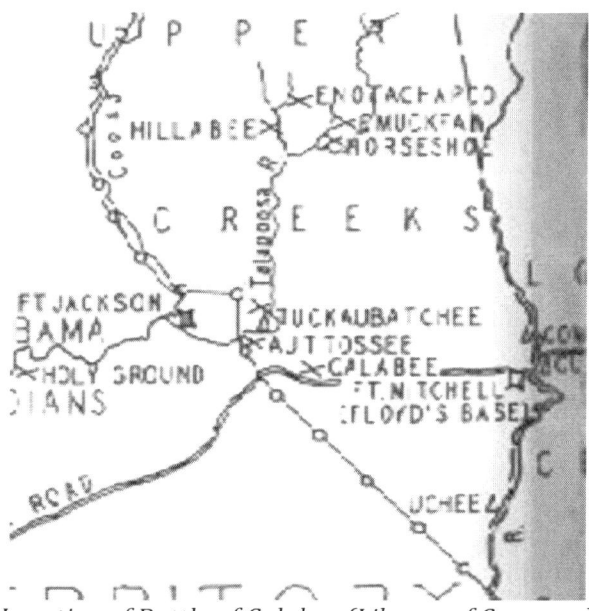

Location of Battle of Calabee (Library of Congress)

News was received that the Indians were fortifying themselves in large numbers at Hoithlewallee on January 26th when General Floyd's troops were encamped in a pine forest, upon the high land bordering Calebee Swamp of present day Macon County, Alabama.

The hostile Red Sticks were encamped in what was subsequently known as McGirth's Still House branch. Here they held a council. Their numbers had increased to 1,800 warriors, probably the largest force assembled during the Creek war. Many were without guns, and were armed with war-clubs, bows and arrows.

Red Eagle, who had been following General Floyd's troop, was present and addressed the council. He proposed that the Indians wait until General Floyd's army had crossed Calebee Creek, but Red Eagle's advice was rejected, and he left the council, and started back to Polecat Spring. About an hour and a half before daybreak on the morning of January 27th, the Indians stealthily approached Floyd's camp, with the Red Stick leader Paddy Welsh directing the attack.

They fired upon the sentinels and made a fierce rush upon the main body. A general action immediately followed. Although surprised, General Floyd's troops were quickly organized. Floyd shouted "Cheer up boys, we will give them hell when daylight comes," and with the aid of the cannon repulsed them. The Indians made desperate efforts to capture the cannon, and in consequence the artillerymen suffered very severely. The assault of the warriors was fierce and determined and they held their ground.

Ezekiel M. Attaway, one of the three men with the guns, shouted to his fellow soldiers, "We must not give up the gun, boys. Seize the first weapon you can lay your hands upon, and stick to your post until the last."

Captain Broadnax, in command of a picket post, was cut off from the camp, but refused to surrender. He and his squad cut their way back through the lines to safety with the assistance of friendly Native American's Timpoochee Barnard and his Uchees. Most of the friendly Native Americans did not participate in the battle.

About daylight Gen. Floyd reorganized his lines, and ordered a general charge. The Indians gave way before the bayonet, and they were pursued through the swamp by Captain Duke Hamilton's cavalry, some of the rifle companies, and by some of the friendly Native Americans. Captain Jett Thomas' artillery company fought bravely in the battle.

The enemies losses are not known, but 70 bodies were found upon the field, including High Head Jim, a major chief and Paddy Welsh was seriously wounded. The American loss was 17 killed, and 132 wounded. The friendly Native Americans loss was 5 killed and 15 wounded.

Floyd's horse was killed under him during the battle. He was sorely hurt, and it was not known how much damage he had inflicted in return, although it is pretty certain that Floyd had greatly the worst of the affair. He held the battlefield, but the Red Sticks were still hovering around his camp and threatening it. It was clear that they believed themselves to be the winners in the action, and that they were preparing to renew it and to crush the Georgia army. Floyd feared they might accomplish this.

The unexpected engagement at Calabee also thwarted Gen. Floyd's designs against Hoithlewallee. He retreated to Fort Hull where he had left a small garrison. Then he returned to Fort Mitchell. After the withdrawal of General Floyd the Creeks took possession of the battlefield.

It is said that Zachariah McGirth—whom we previously mentioned as a survivor of the Fort Mims massacre, and later became a dispatch-bearer, dared all manner of dangers and arrived at Floyd's headquarters on the night of the attack with a dispatch from Claiborne. He had passed through the swamp when it was filled with the enemy awaiting the moment of attack.

The War Ends

Horseshoe Bend

The last and decisive engagement between the Creek Indians and the United States forces under General Andrew Jackson was fought at Horseshoe Bend in what is now Tallapoosa County on March 27, 1814.

For two months General Jackson had been increasing his forces and assembling supplies. The Red Sticks throughout the Nation rallied to a strong native defensive situation on the Tallapoosa River, known as Horseshoe Bend for a final stand. The Native Americans called it Cholocco Litabixee meaning a "horse's flat foot." The place had still another name, Tohope-ka, meaning a "wooden fence," that is, "a fenced off place, a fort."

Horseshoe Bend Marker (Alabama Department of Archives and History)

At Fort Strother on March 1, 1814 General Jackson had an effective force of 4,000 men. This force consisted of the Thirty-Ninth United States Infantry, commanded by Lieutenant Colonel John Williams, General

Johnston's brigade of West Tennesseans, General Dougherty's brigade of East Tennesseans, and General Coffee's mounted rifles with an indefinite number of Cherokees and friendly Creeks. A wagon road had been opened over the divide between the Tennessee River and the headwaters of the Coosa, so that now supplies came to the army in such quantities that full rations were issued regularly to the troops with a surplus of ten days or more ahead.

About two weeks prior to this time, General Jackson was informed by the Kailaidshl chiefs that the Yufaules, the Niuyakas, the Okfuskis, and the remnant of the Hillabees with many hostiles from other quarters, numbering 900 to 1,000, were concentrating in Horseshoe Bend, which they were fortifying and were resolved to defend it to the last. Menawa was their head chief.

With this information General Jackson decided to go down the Coosa River to some eligible point, and establish a new depot. Then he planned to march across the country and strike the Indian stronghold. The mouth of Cedar Creek was selected. Flat boats were constructed on which the supplies were placed, and on March 14, the boats in charge of the Thirty-Ninth Regiment, proceeded down the river. On the same day, after leaving 480 men under Colonel Steele to hold Fort Strother and keep open the communication with Tennessee, General Jackson crossed the river with his army, proceeded down the country, and on the 21st reached the mouth of Cedar Creek. He had to wait a day for the arrival of the boats.

In the meantime a depot was built near the mouth of the creek to which was given the name of Fort Williams in honor of the commander of the Thirty-Ninth Regiment. General Jackson garrisoned the place with a detachment of 400 men under Brigadier General Thomas Johnston, which was to serve as a reserve and to keep open the line of communication with Fort Strother.

The detachments at Fort Strother and Fort Williams, together with various other causes, had by this time reduced the army to about 2,400, in which were included General Coffee's 900 mounted riflemen. His artillery now consisted of two cannon, a new three-pounder, and his old six-pounder of Emuckfau and Enitachopco.

On the morning of March 24th, with eight days' rations, General Jackson left Fort Williams and at nightfall on the 26th camped within five miles of Horseshoe Bend. Early the next morning, agreeably to General Jackson's order, General Coffee, with 700 mounted men, and 600 Indian footmen, 500 Cherokees and 100 Creeks, all the Indians commanded by Colonel Gideon Morgan, crossed the Tallapoosa River at the Little Island ford three miles below the bend, and took possession of the river bank.

Meanwhile, General Jackson moved his army forward, and by 10 o'clock it was drawn up in line of battle in front of the Creek breastwork.

Horseshoe Bend (National Park Service)

No place on the Tallapoosa River was better adapted for the construction of an Indian stronghold than the Horseshoe, a name well descriptive of the locality. It was a peninsula formed by a bend of the river, about 100 acres in area.

Across the isthmus or neck of the peninsula, about 350 yards in extent, the Creeks had erected a rampart from 5 to 8 feet high, curving towards the center, composed of large logs laid upon each other. Two ranges of portholes were made in the rampart, which was so constructed that an army approaching it would be exposed to a double and cross fire from the enemy, who would be well protected on the inner side.

During the long time in which General Jackson was detained at Fort

Strother, the Creeks were busy in constructing this massive stronghold, and from its peculiar structure, some historians have hinted that they must have had the assistance of some English engineer. There were but few trees on the high grounds within the enclosure. But along the declivity and along the flat bordering the river, extending from the terminus of the bend above to the terminus below, the large trees had been felled and so arranged that every fallen tree formed a breastwork, which connected with another fallen tree, thus making a continuous breastwork encircling the entire inner bend. At places in the bank of the river artificial caverns were made, from which concealed warriors could fire.

On the low grounds adjacent to the river and in the extreme southern part of the bend, or point of the Horseshoe, was the Creek village, known as Tohopeka, in which were several hundred women and children, and not far off, many canoes lined the river bank.

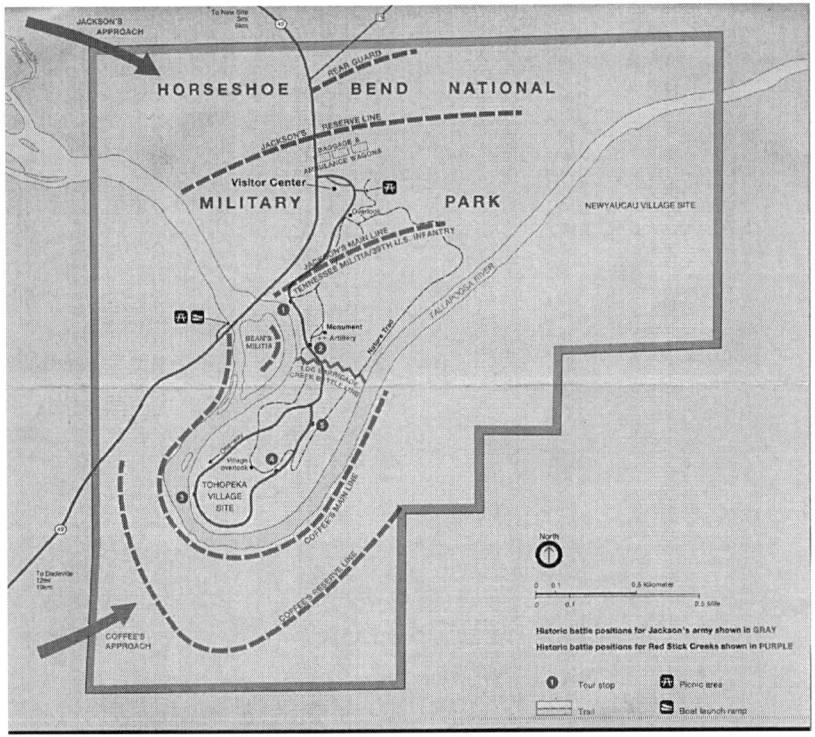

Horseshoe Bend National Park (National Park Service)

Largely ignorant of the overwhelming resources of the white man, encouraged and emboldened by their partial successes at Emuckfau and

Enitachopco at driving General Jackson back to the Coosa River, and the day and night continual religious frenzy by the Red Stick prophets, it can well be seen that the Red Sticks did not believe that this stronghold could be taken. As the Native Americans were always provident and careful of their families in time of war, another evidence of the belief of the Creeks in the impregnability of the place is the fact that when they knew of the coming of the army, yet they did not remove their women and children to some other place where they would be beyond the reach of danger.

About half past 10 o'clock General Jackson planted his cannon on a low hill about 80 yards from the nearest point of the breastwork and about 250 from the farthest, and promptly opened fire upon its center. For two hours, in which 70 rounds were fired, the balls of the two cannon were hurled against the rampart, but they remained unshaken. The cannonading was accompanied at times with the firing of muskets and rifles whenever the Creeks were to be seen behind their breastwork.

During all this time, unaffected by the fire of the cannon and the small arms, the Creeks gave vent to derisive yells, and were assured of the victory by the prophets. The warriors with their faces painted black, their heads and shoulders decorated with feathers, waved their cow tails, jingled their bells, and danced.

In the meantime Gen. Coffee moved up the river, but bearing off for some distance. When about half a mile below, he heard the yells of the Creeks and supposed they were crossing from the village to attack him. He at once formed his men in line of battle and moved forward. When within a quarter of a mile of the village, the firing of Jackson's cannon was heard. Acting according to a previous order, the Cherokees and friendly Creeks immediately rushed forward in good order, took possession of the river bank, and shot some fugitives in the river.

General Coffee now formed his men in line of battle against an attack from the Okfuskee village, some miles below, not knowing at the time that the Okfuskees were in the Bend. About 100 warriors with many women and children could now be seen. This sight, with the continual fire of Jackson's cannon and small arms so aroused the Cherokees and friendly Creeks that some of them plunged into the river, swam across, and brought back a number of canoes. These were at once filled with warriors, rowed across, and landed under cover of the bank, and sent back for reinforcements. In this manner the Cherokees and the friendly Creeks crossed over. Captain Russell's company of spies likewise crossed over.

The river bank was thus left unguarded, and General Coffee placed one-third of his men along around the bend, while two-thirds remained in line in the rear to protect against a possible attack from the Okfuskees.

The attack of the Cherokees and the friendly Creeks upon the rear of the Red Sticks was sufficient to announce to General Jackson that General Coffee had complete possession of the river bank, precluding all hope of escape in that quarter. It was now half past 12 o'clock, and he determined to carry the breastworks by storm, the entire length of which was lined with warriors. The soldiers, regulars, and militia were eager for the assault.

The word was given and the entire line sprang forward. For a few minutes a deadly struggle took place. The muzzles of the opposing guns often met in the same porthole. So close was the fire that afterwards many of the Creek bullets were found lodged and welded fast between the bayonets and barrels of the American muskets.

Major Lemuel Purnell Montgomery of the Thirty-Ninth Regiment was one of the first Americans to fall. He had just shot an Indian with his pistol through a porthole, when an instant after, he fell dead, his head pierced by a bullet coming from the same place.

The breastwork was at last in American possession and the battle now assumed a more deadly aspect.

Everywhere over the peninsula, from behind trees, logs, the tops of fallen timber, and caves in the river bank, from every place that could furnish protection or concealment, assailed by the Americans in front and by the friendly allies in the rear, the Creeks, now hopeless of victory, fought with all the fury of despair. They asked for no quarter and rejected it when offered. It was no longer a battle but a butchery.

Everyone that sought escape by swimming the river became a target for the deadly rifles of Coffee's men. The few that reached the other shore were killed the instant they set foot on land. Bean's company killed every man that approached the island, while Captain Hammond's company was equally destructive at the extremity of the bend above. Many of the Creeks sought the heaps of brush on the west angle of their line of defense, where from their concealment they kept up a constant fire upon the Americans.

General Jackson wishing to save them from utter, destruction and to convince them of the hopelessness of a further struggle, now ordered his interpreter to advance with a flag under the protection of some trees within forty yards of the concealed Indians, and there deliver his talk. The interpreter acted according to instructions. He elevated his voice and spoke in the Native American tongue. He told them of the folly of further resistance, and that he was commanded by General Jackson to say that if they would surrender, they should be duly treated as prisoners of war.

The Creeks listened patiently to the talk of the interpreter, but they remained resolved, and it may be that in that same moment, they bitterly thought of the massacre of the Hillabees, and had no confidence in General Jackson's word. After a few moments pause at the close of the talk, they responded by opening fire upon the flag, by which, whether intentional or otherwise, the interpreter was wounded.

After this, there was no alternative but utter annihilation. After some ineffectual efforts to dislodge them, fire was applied to the brush and thickets, which spreading in every direction drove the Creeks forth and the work of carnage went on.

The Creeks fought everywhere and were slain everywhere, on the high ground, in the caves and along the margin of the river. Night at last put an end to the day's slaughter. The next morning saw the last of the butchery in the killing of sixteen Creeks who had been concealed under the river bank. Of these may be included a small party discovered in a cave in the river bank, and who refused to surrender. The soldiers finding it impossible to dislodge them, finally drove a series of long sharpened stakes deep in the earth along the bluff overlooking the cave. Exerting all their united strength they then pried off the immense mass of earth, which fell and buried the Creeks alive.

The American loss at the Horseshoe was 26 white men killed and 107 wounded. The Cherokees had 18 killed and 36 wounded; the friendly Creeks 5 killed and 11 wounded. The loss of the Red Sticks was fearful, 557 were found and counted on the field. General Coffee estimated that from 250 to 300 were killed in the river. Combining these figures will give at least 800 Creeks killed.

Three prophets were slain, one of these, Monohoe, was shot in the mouth by a cannon ball. General Jackson in writing to Governor Blount four days after the battle, supposed it quite certain that not more than 30 Creeks escaped. Pickett, the Alabama historian, thought it safe to state that about 200 may have survived. Of the survivors was the great chief Menawa, who managed to escape in the darkness of the night. Of the women and children 370 were captured, and according to Buell, about 60 warriors, who were so badly wounded that they could neither fight nor run.

On March 28, 1814, General Jackson buried his dead by sinking them in the river, thereby preventing their mutilation by the Creeks. He had litters made for the transportation of his wounded; then began his return march to Fort Williams, where he arrived on April 1st. Here the friendly Indians were dismissed.

The importance of this battle has been universally recognized by historians, both local and general. A. C. Buell, *History of Andrew Jackson* (1904, Vol. I, p. 338) says:

"This ended the Creek war. For stubborn fighting and for general destruction alike of life and property on the part of the Indians it stands alone in the history of savage warfare on this continent. Never before had the Indians fought in such military fashion, suffered such losses, or held out to the-bitter end as the Creeks did. The fighting power of the tribe was annihilated. At the outbreak of the war the Creeks were the richest Indians in America. At its end they were the poorest. From its disasters they never fully recovered. The destruction of three-fourths of the able-bodied men in any nation or tribe of any race or color must inevitably change its destinies permanently."

The anonymous author of *Memoirs of Andrew Jackson* (1848, p. 122):

"This battle gave a death blow to their hopes, nor did they venture afterwards to make a stand. From their fastness in the woods they had tried their strength, agreeably to their accustomed mode of warfare, in ambuscade, had brought on the attack, and, in all, failure and disaster had been met. None of the advantages incident on surprise, and for which the red men of our forests have always so characterized, had they been able to obtain. The continual defeats they had received were doubtless the reason of their having so strongly fortified this place, where they had determined to perish or to be victorious. Few escaped the carnage. Of the killed many of their friends were thrown into the river whilst the battle raged; many, in endeavoring to pass it, were sunk by the steady fire of Coffee's brigade, and 557 were left dead on the ground. Among the number of the slain were 3 of their prophets. Decorated in a most fantastic manner—the plumage of various birds about their heads and shoulders—with savage grimaces, and horrid contortions of the body, they danced and howled their cantations to the sun. Their dependents already believed a communion with Heaven sure, which, moved by entreaty and their offered homage, would aid them in the conflict and give a triumph to their arms. Fear had no influence, and when they beheld our army approaching and already scaling their line of defense, even then, far from being dispirited, hope survived and victory was still anticipated. Monohoe, one of the most considerable of their inspired ones and who had cheered and kept alive the broken spirit of the nation by his pretended divinations, fell mortally wounded by a cannon shot in the mouth while earnestly engaged in his incantations."

Oh, seldom in the battlefield have fiercer scenes or deadlier strife than this been witnessed. A monument has been erected by the United States Government on the battle ground, as "a memorial to the men who fought in that battle under the command of General Andrew Jackson," at a cost of $5,000. The appropriation was made by act of Congress, April 2, 1914. Congressional action was the direct result of an agitation, begun in 1907 by S. S. Broadus of Decatur. Following an appeal by him the legislature of Alabama created the Horseshoe Bend Battle Anniversary Commission, August 6, 1907. The commission organized and later presented a "Memorial" to Congress, March 3, 1909. Under the auspices of the commission the 100th anniversary of the battle was celebrated by placing a tablet on the courthouse of Tallapoosa County at Dadeville, March 27, 1914, and by a more elaborate celebration on the battle ground itself, July 4, 1914.

The following is the inscription on the tablet:

1814-1914.

This tablet is placed by

TALLAPOOSA COUNTY

in commemoration of the

One hundredth anniversary of the

BATTLE OF HORSESHOE BEND,

fought within its limits on March 27, 1814.

There the Creek Indians, led by Menawa and

[other Chiefs, were defeated by the American and allied

[Indian forces under Gen. Andrew Jackson. This battle broke the power of the fierce

Muscogee, brought peace to the

Southern frontier, and made possible the

speedy opening up of a large part

of the State of Alabama

to civilization.

Dadeville, Alabama,
March 27, 1914.

Monument at Horseshoe Bend (Alabama Department of Archives and History)

The Surrender

The power of the Creek Nation was crushed at the Battle of Horseshoe Bend. Before leaving the Tallapoosa country, entirely which had now become historic, General Jackson took the occasion to plant the American colors on the spot where a century before under the orders of Cadillac had been erected Fort Toulouse when the French were in possession of the country. The old French garrison became the site of new fort manned with a strong block-house and outer walls. The fort received the name Jackson, and it was here that large deputations of Creek warriors constantly came to make formal surrender.

Peter McQueen and Josiah Francis along with several other chiefs fled to Florida, but the greater number of the Creek leaders preferred to remain and sue for Jackson's clemency. To them Jackson replied that he had no further desire to make war, but peace would not be granted to the nation until Red Eagle—or William Weatherford, should be brought to him bound hand and foot. It was his intent to hang Red Eagle as a punishment for the massacre that took place at Fort Mims. General Jackson was unaware of Red Eagle's attempt to make the affair a battle, not a massacre.

Word of Jackson's determination reached Red Eagle and he was encouraged to flee the country and make his escape to Florida. There he would be safe and beyond the jurisdiction of General Jackson and the United States Government, but Weatherford refused. Instead, he mounted his famous gray horse which had carried him over the bluff at Holy Ground, and he rode away alone toward Jackson's camp.

With a daring inconceivable he suddenly appeared at the fort on his splendid charger, with a deer killed on the way swung across his saddle. The daring and utterly fearless Weatherford, dark, sinewy and tall, shrewd and eloquent and handsome, was a most conspicuous figure at the fort.

Though a Creek in every instinct and aspiration, he affected little of the manners and customs of his people. His dress, of the pioneer variety and fashion, had none of the barbaric adornment characteristics.

Surrender of Weatherford to Gen. Jackson, 1814, at Fort Jackson. From an old Engraving.

Wiliam Weatherford surrenders to General Jackson (Library of Congress)

The following account of what took place is from Albert Pickett's *History of Alabama* who stated that it comes from Red Eagle's own narrative in conversations had with him:

He rode within a few miles of Fort Jackson, when a fine deer crossed his path and stopped within shooting distance, which he fired at and killed. Reloading his rifle with two balls, for the purpose of shooting the Big Warrior, should he give him any cause, at the fort, he placed the deer behind his saddle and advanced to the American outposts. Some soldiers, of whom he politely inquired for Jackson's whereabouts, gave him some unsatisfactory and rude replies, when a grayheaded man a few steps beyond pointed him to the marquee. Weatherford rode up to it and checked his horse immediately at the entrance, where sat the Big Warrior, who exultingly (sic) exclaimed:

"Ah! Bill Weatherford, have we got you at last?"

The fearless chieftain cast his keen eyes at the Big Warrior, and said in a determined tone:

"You traitor, if you give me any insolence I will blow a ball through your cowardly heart."

General Jackson now came running out of the marquee with Colonel Hawkins, and in a furious manner exclaimed:

"'How dare you, sir, to ride up to my tent after having murdered the women and children at Fort Mims?"

Weatherford said:

"'General Jackson, I am not afraid of you. I fear no man, for I am a Creek warrior. I have nothing to request in behalf of myself; you can kill me if you desire. But I come to beg you to send for the women and children of the war party, who are now starving in the woods. Their fields and cribs have been destroyed by your people, who have driven them to the woods without an ear of corn. I hope that you will send out parties Who will safely conduct them here, in order that they may be fed. I exerted myself in vain to prevent the massacre of the women and children at Fort Mims. I am now done fighting. The Red Sticks are nearly all killed. If I could fight you any longer I would most heartily do so. Send for the women and children. They never did you any harm. But kill me, if the white people want it done.."

At the conclusion of these words many persons who had surrounded the marquee exclaimed:

"'Kill him! kill him! kill him!."

General Jackson commanded silence, and in an emphatic manner said:

" Any man who would kill as brave a man as this would rob the dead!."

He then invited Weatherford to alight, drank a glass of brandy with him, and entered into a cheerful conversation under his hospitable marquee. Weatherford gave him the deer, and they were then good friends.

Eggleston states that, "Mr. Pickett discredits the accounts of this affair which were given by persons who were present at its occurrence, but they have been accepted by so many writers of repute, including Eaton and Meek, whose opportunities for learning the truth were as good as his, that Mr. Parton regards them as trustworthy at least in their main features."

Following is the remainder of the conversation between Jackson and the heroic chieftain provided by Eggleston as Jackson told Weatherford what terms he had offered to the Creeks, and added:

"As for yourself, if you do not like the terms, no advantage shall be taken of your present surrender. You are at liberty to depart and resume hostilities when you please. But, if you are taken then, your life shall pay the forfeit of your crimes."

Straightening himself up, the bold warrior answered:

"I desire peace for no selfish reasons, but that my nation may be relieved from their sufferings; for, independent of the other consequences of the war, their cattle are destroyed and their women and children destitute of provisions. But I may well be addressed in such language now. There was a time when I had a choice and could have answered you. I have none now. Even hope has ended. Once I could animate my warriors to battle. But I cannot animate the dead. My warriors can no longer hear my voice. Their bones are at Talladega, Tallushatchee, Emuckfau, and Tohopeka. I have not surrendered myself thoughtlessly. While there were chances of success I never left my post nor supplicated peace. But my people are gone, and I now ask peace for my nation and myself. On the miseries and misfortunes brought upon my country I look back with the deepest sorrow, and wish to avert still greater calamities. If I had been left to contend with the Georgia army I would have raised my corn on one bank of the river, and fought them on the other. But your people have destroyed my nation. General Jackson, you are a brave man; I am another. I do not fear to die. But I rely upon your generosity. You will exact no terms of a conquered and helpless people but those to which they should accede. Whatever they may be, it would now be folly and madness to oppose them. If they are opposed, you shall find me among the sternest enforcers of obedience. Those who would still hold out can only be influenced by a mean spirit of revenge. To this they must not and shall not sacrifice the last remnant of their country. You have told us what we may do and be safe. Yours is a good talk, and my nation ought to listen to it. They shall listen to it."

Jackson was too brave a man not to discover the hero in this courageous, self-sacrificing man, who, knowing that an ignominious death had been determined upon for him, calmly refused to save himself, and boldly placed his life in his enemy's hands for the sake of his people. When two men so brave as these meet there is fellowship between them, because there is brotherhood between their souls.

Red Eagle After The War

Having made peace with Red Eagle, Jackson afforded him protection since they were in a camp filled with the friendly Indians, whose hatred of Red Eagle was undying. Big Warrior even tried to take his life in spite of Jackson's orders, and was restrained only by the general's personal interference.

Red Eagle busied himself at once in the pacification of the country, as he had assured Jackson that he would do, and to his great influence, in a large measure, the prompt acquiescence of the Creeks with the terms of peace came about. Afterwards Red Eagle returned to his plantation near Fort Mims to resume his life as a planter, but, his foes among the friendly Native Americans who had sided with the whites were prevalent and that their thirst for his blood made his peaceful stay there impossible.

Weatherford finally went to Fort Claiborne and put himself under the protection of the commanding officer there, who assigned him a tent near his own and a body-guard for his protection. He remained at Fort Claiborne for ten or fifteen days. There were so many persons in the camp who had lost friends at Fort Mims, and who were determined to take the Creek chieftain's life, that his protector feared to keep him at this fort longer.

In the dead of night, Red Eagle was removed in secrecy from Fort Claiborne and taken beyond the camp lines where Captain Laval had arranged to escort him to a tree outside outside the posts. A powerful horse was provided, and Red Eagle, mounted the animal, and galloped away in the darkness to General Jackson's camp.

When he arrived, he was received by the Tennessee general with the respect due a gallant soldier, and there he remained under Jackson's watchful care until after the signing of the treaty of August 9th, 1814, by which the Creeks gave up all the southern part of their territory.

"The treaty was exacted nominally as an indemnity to the government for the expenses of the war, but the real purpose was to plant a strong and continuous line of white settlements between the Creeks and their bad advisers, the Spanish, at Pensacola. By these means Jackson, who managed the affair, made impossible any future renewal of the war to which he had put an end by arms."

"When the treaty was concluded, Jackson's mission was done, and he returned to his Tennessee home—the Hermitage, and took Red Eagle with him as his guest in order that the chieftain might be safe from the assassination with which he was still threatened. Jackson carefully concealed the fact of his presence and for nearly a year the two commanders who had fought each other so fiercely lived together as friends under one roof, the conquered the guest of the conqueror."

Weatherford returned to Alabama, where he established himself as a planter again. His relatives had saved much of his property for him and by wise management he recovered his fortunes and became again a man of considerable wealth.

"Red Eagle had been overcome in war, and was disposed to maintain the peace, in accordance with his promise; but his spirit was not broken, and none of his courage had gone out of him."

"His influence was always on the side of law and order. On one occasion a very brutal assassination was committed at a public sale by two ruffians of the most desperate border type. A magistrate summoned the people as a *posse comitatus* to arrest the offenders, but they so violently swore that they would kill anyone who should approach them. No man dared attempt the duty. Red Eagle, who was present, expressed his indignation at the murder, and his contempt for the fears of the bystanders, and volunteered to make the arrest if ordered by the magistrate to do so."

"The magistrate gave the order, and drawing a long, silver-handled knife, which was his only weapon, Weatherford advanced upon the murderers, who warned him off, swearing that they would kill him if he should advance. Without a sign of hesitation, and with a calm look of resolution in his countenance which appalled even his desperate antagonists, he stepped quickly up to one of them and seized him by the throat, calling to the bystanders to "tie the rascal." Then going up to the other he arrested him, the desperado saying as he approached: "I will not resist you, Billy Weatherford."

Weatherford's plantation was among the white settlements, and the country round about him rapidly filled up with white people, among whom the warrior lived in peace and friendship. Mr. Meek writes of him at this time in these words:

The character of the man seemed to have been changed by the war. He was no longer cruel, vindictive, idle, intemperate, or fond of display: but surrounded by his family he preserved a dignified and retiring demeanor; was industrious, sober, and economical; and was a kind and indulgent master to his servants, of whom he had many. A gentleman who had favorable opportunities of judging says of him that 'in his intercourse with the whites his bearing was marked by nobleness of purpose, and his conduct was always honorable. No man was more fastidious in complying with his engagements. His word was by him held to be more sacred than the most binding legal obligation. Art and dissimulation formed no part of his character. Ever frank and guileless, no one had the more entire confidence of those among whom he lived.

Another gentleman who knew Weatherford intimately for a number of years stated that *"he possessed remarkable intellectual powers; that his perceptions were quick almost to intuition, his memory tenacious, his imagination vivid, his judgment strong and accurate, and his language copious, fluent, and expressive. In short, Weatherford possessed naturally one of the finest minds our country has produced. These traits of character exhibited for a number of years won for their possessor the esteem and respect of those who knew him, notwithstanding the circumstances of his earlier life. Indeed those circumstances threw around the man a romance of character which made him the more attractive. After the bitterness which the war engendered had subsided his narratives were listened to with interest and curiosity. Though unwilling generally to speak of his adventures, he would, when his confidence was obtained, describe them with a graphic particularity and coloring which gave an insight into conditions of life and phases of character of which we can now only see the outside. He always extenuated his conduct at Fort Mims and during the war under the plea that the first transgressions were committed by the white people, and that he was fighting for the liberties of his nation. He also asserted that he was reluctantly forced into the war.*

Red Eagle died on the 9th of March, 1824, from over-fatigue in a bear-hunt. He left a large family of children. Weatherford's nephew, David Moniac, son of his sister, Elizabeth Weatherford, was the first Native American graduate of the United States Military Academy.

Grave of William Weatherford ca. 1930S (Alabama Department of Archives and History)

Graves of Sehoy III and William Weatherford today (Wikipedia)

Bibliography

1. McMaster, John Bach, *A History of the People of the United States,* 1812-1821 D. Appleton, (1915), pp. 162-163

2. Eggleston, George Cary, *Red Eagle: or, Wars with the Indians of Alabama,* Ward, Lock & Company (1881) pp. 70-76

3. Ball, Rev. T. H., *The Great Southeast or Clarke County and its Surroundings,* pub. 1882

4. Riley, *History of Conecuh County* (1881), pp. 16, 62-63

5. Pickett, Albert James *History of Alabama and incidentally of Missspipi and Georgia,* 1896; Mississippi Dept. of Archives

6. Brewer, Rev. George E. *History of Coosa County, Alabama Chapter One* 1872

7. Buell, *History of Andrew Jackson* (1904) Vol 1

8. Brewer, Willis *Alabama, Her History, Resource, War Record and Public Men: from 1540 to 1872*, 1872

9. Jones, Joel D. , "*Old Times*" originally published in *The Democrat Reporter,* Thursday, September 24, 1998

10. Meek, *Romantic passages in southwestern history* (1857), pp, 244-246

11. Claiborne, *Life and times of Sam Dale* (1860), pp. 70-82

12. Halbert and Ball, *Creek War* (1895), pp. 125-142

13. Alabama Historical Reporter, June, 1880

14. Wilson, Thomas, *The Biography of the Principal American,* Applewood Books, Sep. 1, 2009

15. Halbert & Ball, *The Creek War of 1813 and 1814*

16. White, *Historical Collections of Georgia* (1855) pp. 290-292

17. Woodward, *Reminiscences of the Creek Indians* (1859) pp. 101, 102

18. The Atlanta Constitution, April 30, 1905

19. Library of Congress Maps

20. Rowland, Dunbar, Editor, *Publications of the Mississippi Historical*

*Society, Centenary series Volume 4,*1921

21. Snelling, William Joseph, *A brief and impartial history of the life and actions of Andrew Jackson,* Stimpson and Clapp, 1831

Dear Reader,

I hope you enjoyed reading this book as much as I did writing it. To see additional photographs, films and stories about some of the people in this book and other stories of Alabama's history, be sure to visit my website www.alabamapioneers.com.

As an author, I love feedback. I enjoy sharing stories about Alabama's history with you.

I need to ask a favor. Reviews can be tough to come by these days. You, the reader, have the power to make or break a book. If you're so inclined, I'd greatly appreciate a review or simply a comment about *Alabama Footprints - Confrontation* or on any of my books on Amazon.com or Barnes and Noble. I read each one and take them to heart when I write.

You can see all my books on my Author page on Amazon.com at this link. http://www.amazon.com/Donna-R-Causey/e/B0052HE4S0/

In gratitude,
Donna R. Causey

Read more books of the The Alabama Footprints Series

ALABAMA FOOTPRINTS Exploration

ALABAMA FOOTPRINTS Settlement

ALABAMA FOOTPRINTS Pioneers

ALABAMA FOOTPRINTS Confrontation

More coming soon!

Additional information on Alabama can be found on the websites:

www.alabamapioneers.com

www.daysgoneby.me

Follow on Facebook at:

http://www.facebook.com/alabamapioneers

http://www.facebook.com/daysgonebyme

and

Twitter

http://twitter.com/alabamapioneers

Other nonfiction and fictional books by Donna R. Causey can be found
at
Barnes and Noble
or
Amazon.com

Follow Donna R. Causey on

www.facebook.com/alabamapioneers

www.facebook.com/daysgonebyme

http://www.facebook.com/ribbonoflove

or on

Donna R. Causey's websites

www.alabamapioneers.com

www.daysgoneby.me

Made in the USA
Middletown, DE
19 December 2015